Writing

for Trade Magazines

How to Boost Your Income
by $200 to $500 per Week

By Kendall Hanson

Dixon-Price Publishing
Murray, Utah

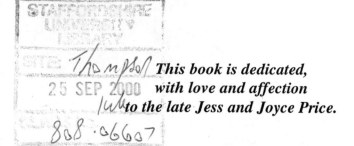
This book is dedicated,
with love and affection
to the late Jess and Joyce Price.

Copyright© 1999 by Kendall Hanson
All rights reserved.

Publisher's Cataloging-in-Print Publication
(Provided by Quality Books, Inc.)

Hanson, Kendall.
    Writing for trade magazines : how to boost your income by $200 to $500 per week / by Kendall Hanson.
    -- 1st ed.
    p. cm.
    Includes bibliographical references and index.
    ISBN: 1-929516-05-3

    1. Journalism, Commercial--Authorship.
    2. Editing. 3. Home-based businesses. I. Title.

PN4784.C7H36 1999   070.4'4965
                     QBI99-1278

Library of Congress Number: 99-091236

Dixon-Price Publishing books are available for special promotions and premiums. For information, contact: Marketing Director

Electronic versions of this book are available. For more information, see the Dixon-Price Publishing web site at http://www.dixon-price.com.

04089924

Acknowledgments

I'd like to take just a brief moment to acknowledge the people who helped to make this project a reality through their comments and support:

Heather Hatfield, The McGraw-Hill Cos.
Sam Barnes, *Louisiana Contractor*
Mark Shaw, *Intermountain Architecture*
Sheila Bacon, *Northwestern Construction*
Joe Evancho, Sr.
Joe Evancho, Jr.
Phil Clark, who made me realize such a book was needed.
Jerry Campbell, past national board member of the American Subcontractors Association
Wayne Bingham, AIA
Ron Hall, past board member of the American Concrete Institute, who reminded me to stop and smell the roses occasionally

I would especially like to thank the people who have had to put up with my writing struggles for all these years: Maureen, Jennifer, Jed, Jessi, and Jake, and Gilbert and Evelyn Hanson.

TABLE OF CONTENTS

How-to stories.
Service stories.
Write in chapters.
Where to find how-to and service story ideas.
Self-help articles.

Writing the round-up story.
Getting started on the trend story.
How many sources?
Organize the story.
How to organize your research.
Make an evaluation.
Special notes about trade shows.
Is news viable?
Profiles outside the editorial well.
The open door for expers.
What about consumer magazines?
Help yourself by learning to file.
Single project files.
Keeping track of projects and deadlines.
Keeping track of what you owe and what's owed to
you.
A brief aside on copyrights.
Don't just show me the money, show me where it
goes.
Managing your daily work.
Start with good planning.
The first editorial sweep—completing the rough draft.
The second sweep—a "baseline" edit.
The long third sweep—find the peccadillos.
A last quick sweep.
Research once, write often.
Give yourself a raise?
Is there a book?
How do copyright laws affect you in a rapidly chang-
ing industry?

Preface

This book has been written for three kinds of people:

Writers who want to supplement their income while they build their path to full-time freelancing.

Young writers, maybe still in school, who want to get that first "break" or sell their first article.

Professionals and craftsmen, retired or wanting to retire, who want to translate their accumulated knowledge and skill into a supplemental income.

Writing articles for trade magazines can do all three. I always think about the words of the angry coach in the movie *Bull Durhan*: "It's a simple game. You throw the ball. You hit the ball. You catch the ball!"

Like many writers, I came to trade journalism in a very roundabout way after writing several short plays, television scripts, and other fiction works that have yet to see the light of day. Ten years of this dabbling and a corporate restructuring finally convinced me it was time to find a job that would make better use of my degree in English and the time I had lavished in college learning to string words together to communicate.

An opportunity came with McGraw-Hill's F.W. Dodge division which collects data about commercial construction. For a little over a year, I called an average of fifteen to twenty architects and contractors per day, took down the details of the projects they were working on, and fit those details into a formatted report.

The job was much more fun than it sounds. I developed a rapport with many of these professionals that continues today. I also developed a respect, not only for the depth of their knowledge about their industry, but also for the passion of their commitment to craftsmanship, professionalism, and execution.

I was stunned. I had experienced just a few individuals with this high level of passion and *excitement* before in the better college professors I had known and in a *few* professional writers and artists. All of a sudden, here was an industry filled with people who not only enjoyed their work, but were addicted to it. Suddenly it all became clear: "It's a simple game. Writers write. Builders build. Designers design."

When the opportunity came to freelance a couple of articles for a regional magazine on construction that McGraw-Hill had just bought, I jumped on it although my last experience with "journalism" had been with the student newspaper in college.

A position opened suddenly; I was asked to apply and got the job. For nine years I honed my skills, more in interviewing and networking than in the actual ability to communicate with words on paper although that improved as well. In 1998, during an interview with a prominent local contractor who was talking about the joy that building's challenges gave him, I realized it was time to move to another level in my own career and decided to become a freelance writer.

My hope is that this book will provide a guide for you to start your writing career if you haven't done so already; and if you have, but are finding many of the doors of opportunity closed, I hope this book will renew your determination by offering one more, very large, door to try. All I can promise is that you will get out of trade journalism what you put into it.

Kendall Hanson
Salt Lake City

Chapter 1

What you absolutely must know about trade magazines but were never taught in school—and why.

The benefits of writing for trade magazines

Trade magazines pay as well or better than general interest magazines. A myth has long existed, I think, that trade magazines don't pay as well as their better known sisters. I've never written for any trade magazine for less than $300 an article, find that most pay between 25 and 35 cents a word—at this writing roughly a dime higher than most of the general interest magazines I know of, or about an extra $100 per thousand words of copy if you want to think of it that way. In fact, on some assignments I've seen my copy go for as much as $2 per word, and I'm hard pressed to think of more than a handful of general interest magazines which pay that well.

Trade magazines are relatively easy to break into. Imagine you are the articles editor for Ladies Home Journal. How many query letters do you receive in a single day? How many unsolicited manuscripts? Fifty? A hundred? Multiply that by two hundred and twenty working days a year. No wonder those editors take work home at night and on the weekends. Even with assistants, how do you screen all of that material?

Now compare that with a recent cold call I had with the editor of magazine covering the audio/visual industry:

"Freelance?" Long pause. "I don't think anyone's every asked me before. Yeah, I suppose we would use some freelance if it fit our magazine. What's the story?"

I name three, all installations of audio/visual systems in local office and business projects under construction.

"Yeah, those sound great. Those would work in our "System" sections. When can you send them?"

Quite a difference from the standard form rejection from *Family Circle* which arrives three or four months after you query.

We quickly get into a discussion about the pay for these articles which, admittedly, are on spec—but not really because I already have looked at the magazine and know exactly what is wanted for the "System" section. The agreed price is slightly less than what I would receive by writing the same length pieces for *Family Circle*. But considering the time and effort I would waste sending a query, waiting six to eight weeks for a potential reply, and then putting together the article, probably on spec anyway, my spec assignments from this trade magazine are almost like money in the hand. By the way, they paid on acceptance.

Not all trade magazines are quite so easy to break into, but the vast majority compare more than favorably with their consumer-oriented cousins.

Trade magazine editors tend to be loyal. One of the by-products of having few freelancers providing stories for trade magazines is that most trade magazine editors are very loyal to their freelancers. I don't mean to imply that consumer magazine editors can't be just as loyal, just that, again, the narrow market of good trade writers means that trade editors often don't have any back-up writer waiting in the wings.

For good reason. Writing for a trade magazine, as you'll

learn in these pages, has an added element that favors writers willing to spend the time and effort necessary to learn an industry's needs and issues. The basic truth for a trade writer is that the writer is not a member of the audience he's writing for.

Think of that implication. If you write for a newspaper, you generally can count yourself as one member of its vast general audience. If you write for a shelter magazine, and live in a house or an apartment, then you can count yourself a member of that magazine's potential audience. You already know in a visceral sense what that audience wants to know about, what topics are of interest, what topics are old hat, and what material within a particular topic is most important.

Unless you are an audio engineer or a subcontractor who installs A/V systems, you don't know what's important to your audience in *Systems Contractor News* because you aren't a member of that audience. Don't despair, though. I'll show you how to find out what's important to a trade audience within these pages. Once you understand how to act on this simple secret, you'll be able to go forth and tackle any type of trade magazine subject.

Trade magazine writing provides a base of research that can be used in crossover articles for consumer magazines and newspapers. One of the great benefits of writing for trade magazines is the spillover effect of a potential topic into the more traditional channels of consumer periodicals. There are hundreds of ways to reconfigure most basic research in a trade article to appeal to a consumer audience. Let me give you an example. Recently I came across a young man who was building post-and-beam buildings using an updated version of the oak-pegged mortise-and-tenon construction our founding fathers used to build their homes and their barns.

The potential sales of this article floored me. First, it was easily possible to pitch an article to a regional trade magazine. At the same time, it made sense to pitch the article to a national magazine for commercial architects who design facili-

ties for winter resorts (and often crossover into high-end cus-
tom homes at the adjoining housing developments). Since the
builder was using pre-engineered wood (joists and beams made
from strips of wood pressure-glued together), it was also possible to pitch the story to a construction industry environmental trade magazine (yes, there is such a thing, several in fact) as
well as a wood industry magazine. The likelihood of these
magazines competing directly with each other was slim.

Next, I could reslant the article to the consumer market
for those who are thinking about building their own home.
Could have gone to a national magazine, but I opted instead
to self-syndicate the article to regional daily newspapers. Once
I'm sure those dailies who want the story have run them, I'll
can recirculate the article to weekly newspapers.

But we aren't done yet. As long as the article is interesting
to home owners in the U.S., what about home owners in En-
gland? Australia? Switzerland? As far as that goes, lets query
the same types of trade magazines in every language we can
find. Why? Because most are willing to interpret the article for
you.

If you think about the possibilities inherent in reselling
articles and reslanting your basic research, it becomes obvious
that writing for trade magazines offers a virtual gold mine for
the magazine writer. Magazine articles all have the same basic
characteristics:

1. Contacts that are quoted.
2. Facts that are cited.
3 A human interest angle.
4. A defined or implied trend.

Trade writing still requires the same dedication to good
writing that you would find in consumer-oriented publications.
In some ways writing a good trade magazine feature is even
more challenging and satisfying than writing a similar piece
for a consumer periodical.

What trade magazines are

Today, trade magazines are prospering, and in many ways are more prosperous than their consumer-oriented relatives because their mission is one that will be ongoing for some time. Trade magazines are:

News providers. The foremost function for most trade magazines is to provide news for the industry they serve, including news about products, services and techniques that can help businesses within the industry either prosper or avoid loss.

Marketplaces. There is no doubt that almost all trade magazines view themselves first and foremost as a marketplace where supplier can reach user. The essential financial fact of modern magazines, trade or otherwise, is that advertising revenue is what keeps the magazine in business. But in addition to advertising, most editors realize that information on new sources of supplies or new innovations in equipment or services available are vital for keeping businesses competitive and vital.

A forum for important issues. People within an industry must come together to share ideas, or the industry as a whole will fall behind in providing the right goods and services to match the changes in society. Debate in an industry is healthy—it shakes up the thinking and lets new solutions emerge.

In the construction industry, for example, debate about the cost of environmentally sensitive construction versus cost-effective construction has gradually changed the way marketers talk to owners, often emphasizing the lifetime cost of a building, including maintenance and utility costs, which often are much less when a little more money is spent in making the building environmentally sensitive.

Initially, environmental sensitivity in construction had few supporters within the construction industry, but as I've watched it progress over a nine-year span, more and more general contractors, subs, and suppliers have realized that not only do they feel good about building that way, they also can maintain their profits and even reduce their costs in many instances.

Idea generators. While you can't truly say there is nothing new under the sun, you can say there is very little. Trade magazines are marketplaces not just for goods, but for ideas. In the example above, the environmental debate showed how an industry can shift. In my area of the country, however, one architect has had a tremendous influence on his industry. He insisted the firm's design for every project be as energy efficient as possible and maximize natural light.

Naturally, this saved money for building owners, so the firm grew apace. Other firms noticed, and started emphasizing energy efficiency too. Now this trend is in full swing within the region, and judging by the articles I've seen in design magazines, it is a trend that's gone national.

As it happened, I've had my own small part to play, first reporting in a regional magazine on a government facility the firm had designed. Next I saw a national magazine do its own version of a story on the facility, and then other similar projects made their way into a variety of national trade magazines during the next several years.

In fact, trade magazines are also idea generators for the consumer press as well. Many trends first get noticed in the trade press, so it is a wise journalist who looks to trade magazines for consumer story ideas.

Watchdogs. A very real myth exists that trade magazines won't take on difficult topics that might cost them advertisers. Although trade magazines are first and foremost loyal to the industries they serve, much like an association, that loyalty is tempered with an understanding that honest practices serve everyone's long term interests. Every industry, it seems, has its own set of "sharp" practices that may be within the limits of the law but are frowned upon.

Trade magazines, however, have a good history of exposing fraudulent practices and decrying the worst of the sharp practices. Although a trade magazine's first duty isn't to be a member of the ethics police, in the everyday pursuit of stories, most editors get to know the industry intimately, get to know what is acceptable and what is beyond the excessive in either a legal or ethical sense, and will often use the bully pulpit to bring abuses to task for the good of the industry.

On the other end of the spectrum, however, the freelancer should approach controversial story suggestions with caution. If trade magazines are often watchdogs, they are often apologists as well. It's possible to condemn an industry practice without condemning the industry, and freelance writers who want to work on more investigative stories should remember that. If a story is going to uncover, say, an industry-wide practice whose scope is harmful outside the industry, a general publication is probably a better format, especially if such a practice is considered ethical and common within the industry.

What happens, of course, is that industries are run by human beings who, after all, tend to put blinders on when their best interests are threatened. A good example, in my estimation, was the spotted owl controversy in Oregon a few years ago. The construction industry was up in arms at first because they perceived a major source of lumber—and thus their means of supplying production—would be cut off. But a response to such a situation had already been growing, the production of "pre-engineered" lumber made by gluing fragments of wood together to make beams, I-joists and even wood studs and molding.

The result, ultimately, was that the industry learned to replace the old materials with the new technology, and discovered in the process the shift was both good for the industry—for the new wood produces a truer wall, better support for roof and floor, and is quicker to install—and good for the environment. Once again an industry's ethics had been notched up a level, willingly or not.

"Community newspapers" for an industry. People move, they get promoted, they receive awards, they retire, they pass away.

Companies move, their products change, their management changes, their scope changes. In a very real sense, an industry becomes a "community" as well as a place to work for most people who get to know colleagues and competitors alike in their daily work. Trade magazines help them keep track of each other over the years.

What trade magazines are not

It's tempting to lump in various profit centers that may be adjunct to a trade magazine as part of the trade magazine "market," but in practice writers will find that there are few opportunities for them there.

Some publications often appear analogous to trade magazines, but aren't trying to fulfill the same functions. For example:

Technical journals. From a freelance writer's standpoint, technical journals offer only a limited opportunity and that is to co-author an article or "ghost" it for an expert in the particular field. Technical journals fulfill a much needed role—continuing education and a forum for ideas—but don't include many of the other functions of a true trade magazine such as providing a marketplace and serving as a community newspaper.

Also, technical journals seldom pay their contributors except in copies. Since their primary function is educational, they are looking for contributed articles from scholars or working experts within the field. Typically these articles go into much more depth and are much more technical than would be found in a trade magazine, because the audience for a technical journal is most often a small group of experts involved in that particular field or those in related fields who must have some crossover knowledge of the subject.

One way of distinguishing between a journal and a magazine is to count the number of advertisements. While some prominent journals have begun to accept advertising in the last 20 years, most still depend on subscriptions for their main income instead of relying on advertising revenues. That fact alone tends to keep their circulation small because few subscriptions are sold to those outside the field.

Newsletters. Newsletters can offer some potential for freelancers, but their function is almost the opposite of a journal's though frequently targeted to much the same limited-focus audience. Rather than go in depth, however, as a journal does, a newsletter's function is to give the most up to the minute information or view in a particular subject.

In practice, say, a food engineering journal might have a 5,000 word article on detecting and eliminating a certain bacteria within a certain process for producing chocolate flavored yogurt including detailed directions or measures so that another food engineer can duplicate the experiment or process. In the newsletter, the 300-word article would mention that such a process exists, that so and so have tried it successfully, and that more information can be found at such and such a place. Or it might report that a new group has formed to support each other educationally to make this an industry-wide standard—in short, the news of the subject, not the subject itself.

Directories and data services. Directories and data services are a natural outgrowth of the trade magazine business because to remain successful with circulation—and thus advertising—a publication must always be accumulating and updating various lists. Subscribers. Advertisers. Potential advertisers. Potential subscribers. As long as a publisher has people doing that kind of work anyway, why not make a little extra profit selling those lists to others who need them? However, directory publishing and data services, while useful to freelancers who need to know who is where, seldom offers any direct opportunity to sell articles.

The one exception is when a company decides to do a combined piece that includes both written articles and directories. Sometimes these become special issues. *Remodeling,* for instance, will publish a directory of suppliers in a once a year special issue, and the issue will also contain some articles. In most cases, however, most of the material is generated by the magazine's staff or contributing editors.

Occasionally, some publishers put together such a combined directory/magazine as a separate piece. *Engineering News-Record*, for example, bundles its survey of the nation's top contractors, a directory of their addresses and phone, together with articles on the health and future of various construction markets, and put that bundle of related information into a supplement sold separately as *The Top 400 Contractors Sourcebook*. While *ENR* and *Remodeling* have sufficient staff to do these publications in-house, not all trade magazines that publish such directories have the staff to accomplish this, so there are a few scattered opportunities to write articles around such a service.

Borderline publications. Some publications are hard to classify as either trade magazines or trade journals. Two that come to mind are *Fire Chief* and *American Jails*. On the one hand, each carries a variety of industry news on issues, people, events; provides a marketplace; provides a forum for the discussion of issues; and without a doubt are publications where new ideas can be generated.

On the other, most, if not all, of the articles published are solicited from experts in the field and peer-reviewed with the intention of providing continuing technical education on narrowly focused subjects, and from that perspective, a freelancer's opportunities are limited to much the same options as a trade journal. If you do see an article recognizable as a "feature," it is almost always written in-house.

How big is the trade magazine industry?

It's difficult to measure how large the trade magazine industry is. No single directory seems capable of listing all of the trade magazines which exist. One of the best sources for finding trade magazines is Standard Rates & Data Service's *Business*

Rates and Data which lists around 4,500 magazines. When you look at volume three, however, which deals just with publications in the healthcare field, both magazines and journals that accept advertising, you probably add another 500 purely "trade" magazines as well as 500 technical journals.

Although *Business Rates and Data* is a place to start, it is by no means definitive on the subject of trade magazines. During the years I was editor for three trade magazines produced by McGraw-Hill, none of the three ever appeared in the SRDS. Those three magazines were part of a network of regional construction magazines known as the Construction News Publishing Network (now known as Dodge Construction Publications) which totaled fourteen different magazines, only one of which ever appeared in SRDS because a listing there requires an audited circulation figure.

Auditing circulation is an expense many smaller magazines see no justification for. In Intermountain Contractor's case, the publication's actual circulation was only about 3,500 subscribers. In practice, however, the weekly magazine was passed around an office because of the detailed news it gave on projects in planning and projects out for bid. At a medium-sized construction office, perhaps five estimators plus the marketing manager and president would look at the magazine each week. IC claimed an actual readership of 10,000, and my personal experience tells me that figure was on the conservative side. But since there is no reliable way to audit "pass around," but only actual subscribers, it wasn't in the magazines interest to spend the money. With its long tradition in the area, no advertisers ever blinked at this situation.

One way to estimate the potential number of trade magazines is to look at the amount of six-digit SIC (Standard Identification Code) numbers that businesses are divided into. SICs classify industries, and as already noted, most industries have one or more trade magazines serving them. As I look at a recent directory of mailing lists sent to me, for example, I check the first entries for "E". I've never seen a magazine specifically for Ear Piercing Service (7299-28), but there may be one. I do know there is a magazine as well as a couple of newsletters that serve the Earthquake Products & Services (1799-78) sector, a trade magazine for Eating Disorders Information and Treatment Centers (8049-31), several for Eating Places (i.e. Restaurants—5812-08), a good one for Eaves & Troughs (1761-03), and at least two that I know of for Economic Development Agencies (8748-75).

If I were to hazard a guess in print, which I will, my instinct tells me that in 1998 in the U.S. alone there were probably a few more than 8,000 trade magazines accepting advertising, and if you expand that definition to include those journals and newsletters that accept either occasional advertising or the occasional freelance article, the number of potential markets would probably jump to about 13,000.

On the international scene, it becomes even more difficult to isolate a particular number. Uhlrich's Guide to World Periodicals lists about 17,000 trade magazines, including many in the U.S. It's not so broad a list as the SRDS, but again, my years of experience tell me that figure is probably low and more likely the figure is closer to 20,000 or more worldwide if you include the international editions published by North American publishers. Surprisingly, *Intermountain Contractor* was listed in the edition I checked.

Remember, trade magazines have as many profit/loss difficulties as consumer-oriented magazines, and while their mortality rate is somewhat lower, they can still die off. As we develop the notion about who the audience is for a trade magazine, you'll see that when an industry shifts, it can cause the magazine to go under regardless of the quality of the editorial product.

How trade magazines define their audience

The starting point for any writer is to understand the audience to write for. For trade magazines, as for any other publishing concern, an audience is made up of readers who share similar interests and goals. Inseparable from an understanding of the broad audience is an understanding that you are also writing for one specific person: the editor. It's necessary, therefore, to understand how a trade magazine "positions" itself.

I would submit that most—though certainly not all—trade magazines will target one of what I call the "Big Three" groups: manufacturers, wholesalers, or retailers. Another way to look at this breakdown is as a simple supplier/user continuum. When you have a supplier and a user, you have a marketplace.

In construction, for example, the material supplier's end user is the contractor. The contractor's end user is the owner. One group is always trying to "reach" the other and therein lies the justification for advertising. In healthcare, the biomedical manufacturer is the supplier, the healthcare professional is the user. In the travel industry, the airline or the rental car agency or the hotel is the supplier, the travel agent is the user, or more specifically, the gatekeeper to the user.

Most industries have a manufacturer who sells the product to a wholesaler, a wholesaler or distributor who then re-sells the product to a retailer, and then the retailer sells the product to a consumer. That simple process is breaking down in many industries even as I write for a variety of reasons. Changes in technology allow manufacturers to take their product directly to a retailer more cost effectively than had been possible in the past.

To get a good handle on what types of articles a trade magazine editor may want, you must look at who they are trying to reach how. Here's how do it.

By the type of circulation. Magazines always have a simple choice: Paid subscriptions or free subscriptions. Charging nothing is called a "closed circulation." For a variety of reasons, many trade magazines charge nothing for subscriptions. In the case of magazines produced by associations, the cost of the subscription is often buried in the dues structure. For most trade magazines, the cost of producing and mailing to a targeted group is inherent in the price for advertising.

Just because a magazine uses controlled (i.e. free) circulation, it doesn't mean that the editorial standards are necessarily lax. What it does generally mean, however, is that the magazine uses a minimum of expensive staff for production and frequently outsources for writing as well as other services— good news for you. At the same time, a controlled circulation also means you must absolutely focus on the needs and wants of the reader they are trying to reach.

Even full subscription magazines have their share of complimentary copies going out. Understand that a full subscription magazine still derives the majority of its revenue through advertising (unless it is a true journal). For the most part, subscription based audiences tend to be broader in scope than controlled circulations because they will often include subscribers who have a peripheral interest in the field as well as those who are specific to it. This doesn't change your responsibility to target the right reader, but it does mean there will often be a broader range of topics considered by the editor of this type of magazine.

By subscriber type. First and foremost, trade magazines exist to reach a specific type of reader within an industry. In construction, for instance, you can generally look at a book and tell immediately whether it is intended for building owners, contractors, designers or suppliers. The actual field is almost superimposed over this industry breakdown. Thus a magazine may be designed to be read by, say, contractors in the audio/visual field, such as *Systems Contractor News*. The readers are A/V contractors and A/V engineers. The advertisers are producers and wholesalers of A/V equipment. You can generally develop a vertical hierarchy that gives you a sense of who you are writing for and whose money is driving the ad revenue.

If a book is designed for a certain category of building owner, then the contractors, designers, and suppliers will be interested in reaching that owner through both advertising and stories. If the magazine is for contractors, a few kinds of designers will be interested in reaching that readership and almost all suppliers. Why the designers? Because in construction nowadays, the design/build method of delivering projects means that contractors instead of owners are now hiring the designers. This approach is being seen in other industries as well where production and design have been separate in the past. The reverse is also true. In magazines for designers, particularly architects, contractors who perform design/build projects like to get their name in front of the architectural firms because in the standard process of commercial construction, designers are most likely to hear about a particular project first because the owner contacts them in the preliminary stages to help determine how much space will be needed.

In most types of industries where a product is produced rather than a service, there will be magazines serving a vertical hierarchy such as this, i.e. an "owners" or end users magazine, a wholesaler/distributor/supplier magazine, and a manufacturer's magazine. There can be different levels of manufacturers as well, generally as a number of components are needed to make the final product. Again in the construction analogy, there's a manufacturer of framing lumber at one level, providing a component through a distributor to the final manufacturer, the general contractor. Each rung on the ladder is trying to reach the next rung up, but often there are some advantages for the rung up to reach down as well. For example, a manufacturer's rep who wants to expand the lines he represents may advertise in a manufacturer's magazine.

Service hierarchies tend to be slightly different. Service companies often need both products and other service companies. An advertising firm may use outside design services, or outside market research services, or outside video production services, or outside mailing services. It will also need more concrete products such as printed brochures, photographic duplicates, etc. So while there is a manufacturer-distributor linkage for some elements, there is more often a direct "manufacturer"-user linkage.

By direction. We have been talking about the vertical nature of the trade audience, but there are also horizontal magazines. These are often based on professional positions or management areas that cut across industry lines such as accounting, safety management, contract management, food service management, database management, etc. Products or professions or trades that cut across industry lines.

As Patrick Clinton notes in *Guide to Writing for the Business Press*, covering multiple segments of an industry is a horizontal strategy. In a magazine where both vertical and horizontal coverage is wide-spread, the magazine can tend to take on the nature almost of a "generalized" niche publication, an oxymoron that actually makes some sense in practice.

For a magazine such as *Engineering News-Record*, which seeks to cover the broadest range of subjects within the commercial construction industry, it's hard to feel any vertical tug in the editorial direction although maybe the best way to categorize that tug is to say the magazine serves construction industry company owners. To do that, *ENR* concentrates primarily on news, trends, and broad service articles, with an occasional company or personal profile thrown in—a mix strategy you will find in magazines that seek to cover the entire scope of an industry.

By industry function. While there are magazines such as *ENR* which take a broad look at an industry's business issues, there are also trade magazines that look at just one function within an industry, generally in management, marketing, maintenance, purchasing, data management, or safety.

By location. Many trade magazines exist to serve an industry in a particular region. Sometimes these magazines field a wide range of industry issues, but concentrate on how those issues play out within their region. *Intermountain Contractor*, which I was privileged to edit for many years, tried to strike a balance between building and engineering construction within Utah and the immediate areas bordering it. *UTAD News* covers the "media" industry in the Salt Lake metropolitan area, including radio and television, print, advertising agencies, public relations, video production, and virtually any element that makes up the promotion industry in the area.

Regional trade magazines offer a good opportunity for a freelance writer to break in. If staff is now spread thin at national magazines, it has practically melted into the toast at regional magazines. During most of the time I was editor at *IC*, I was also producing articles for—and finally editing—*Intermountain Architecture*. At the same time, I was also editing *Utah Building Magazine*, a monthly for the residential industry, and edited about forty of the fifty-two issues per year *of Intermountain Contractor News Weekly*. From the time I began as editor in January of 1990 until the organization was restructured in January 1997, I had exactly two—two!—freelance queries.

One of the benefits of writing for a regional trade magazine is also the quick access it gives you to experts within your region. All industries are, in a sense, regional, so generally those folks who are good at what they do understand how beneficial it is for their name to appear in the region's trade magazine as well as in national publications. Some actually prefer the regional coverage over the national because their customers are in the region.

Trade magazine publishing is a growth cycle industry

On of the most interesting aspects of trade magazines is how they are tied to the growth of an industry. In the late 1960s, for example, you would have searched long and hard to find any trade magazine devoted exclusively to computers or the computer industry. By the mid-1980s, such magazines were much more plentiful, but just fifteen years later, more than 100 national trade magazines are devoted to one aspect or another of the computer industry, and virtually all trade magazines across the board will have an occasional article on how computers are affecting their industry and changing its face.

For that matter, the growth of trade magazines has proliferated thanks to technology and science in general which create new industries almost every day. Satellites may watch over potential enemies, for instance, but they also make your pager beep and feed your favorite soap opera into the local television station for retransmission even as they help surveyors plot the land. Each of those functions has built up its own industry, complete with manufacturers, wholesalers, and retailers or representatives.

The way markets "become" is interesting in itself. Al Reis and Jack Trout identified an interesting phenomenon in the 1970s in their book, *The 22 Immutable Laws of Marketing*. For years IBM was synonymous with the word "computer." Now computer in the 1970s meant anything from a big mainframe to the relatively new PET personal computer. Along came a very smart man, Steven Jobs, who developed a computer with his friends. Realizing they would never be able to compete head to head with IBM, they decided to create a new category: "Personal" computer. Voila, a new industry was launched.

What's important about the growth of new industries for trade magazine publishers is the understanding that new trade magazines *must* target specific niches. It's not a great intellectual stretch to understand why. In fledgling industries, there are few advertisers and possibly few readers. To be successful, trade magazines must deliver a coherent group of readers an advertiser wants to reach.

If you are manufacturing magnetic imaging devices for medical diagnoses, you need to advertise to hospital administrators and the doctors who serve on the advisory panels. You don't need to reach the nurse on the ward, the operating room orderly, or even the family practice physician (journals will take care of that task).

Advertising dollars drive the trade magazine industry. What that means for the writer is that there are always two audiences that you are basically writing for. First and foremost is certainly a magazine's reader. No one disputes that. But the nature of the trade magazine industry is such that you are also writing somewhat for the ad salesman. In so far as your story reaches the magazine's reader, you have provided the service that's needed, but it's important to understand that in many situations, the editor must "sell" your story to the advertising staff.

In most consumer publications, and generally within newspapers, there's a tacit "firewall" between the editorial and the sales department. In trade magazines such as *Engineering News-Record* where content focuses on news across a broad industry range this division still holds fairly true.

The more targeted the magazine's editorial mix and geographic location, however, the more input most advertising departments have on the editor's choice of stories. That's not to say that editors will pass up a good story, but it is to warn the potential freelancer that having a hook ad reps to sell to, as well as an interesting story slant, is becoming more and more important in the trade magazine market.

The challenge for the freelance writer

The most fundamental truth about writing for trade magazines is that the writer is seldom, if ever, the same as the audience. That basic fact is both the challenge and the excitement of writing for the trades.

With trade magazines, however, familiarity with a subject based at least in part on being a member of the audience is minimized. If you are a writer who plans to write for *Restaurants & Institutions*, *Facility Management*, and *Environmental Design and Construction*, chances are you *could* be a member of one of the audiences, but certainly not the other two.

In fact, if your training is primarily in writing, you will have almost no understanding of the audience for a particular trade magazine because trade magazines deal in specific information, not general information. You are out of the loop when it comes to professional understanding, although if you work within a field for a long time, you'll likely pick up a sense of the industry which makes you somewhat a part of the audience.

To start off, though, the first challenge for the freelance writer is to find a mentor, a member of the industry who can advise you about issues and give you some direction.

That may be why writing for trade magazines gets such short shrift in journalism schools. Uncovering information of use in everyday life is relatively uncomplicated, so study assignments which develop particular skills are easier to make. Uncovering information of use within a particular business industry involves developing very specialized knowledge, including specialized contacts. At the same time, writing for trade magazines opens up so many more opportunities for a writer that it's difficult to understand why more emphasis isn't put into the subject.

In the final analysis, writing for trade magazines has many of the same challenges as writing for general publications plus a few more. But the rewards in profitability and the opportunity to broaden your scope of understanding about how the world operates make trade writing a valuable supplement to developing a career.

Chapter 2

What trade editors want; what they actually need; and why you are the best person to provide both.

What trade editors care about.

In the most basic ways, trade magazine editors are no different than their counterparts in the consumer press. They want articles that give beneficial information to their readership. They want high quality writing with a sense of style as well as strong, accurate content. They understand that good writing insures readers will read and that the fundamental job of any editor is to make sure the magazine is read.

In an age where information seemingly can be found almost everywhere at once, trade editors more and more understand what consumer editors have known for some time: To keep a readership coming back for more, you must occasionally "refresh" your magazine's content, if not in general topicality, then in the style of writing that provides the information. One of the fundamental reasons freelance writers can be of great benefit to a trade magazine is because they bring a fresh approach, a new way of looking at a topic or a new way of thinking about an issue.

Refreshing a magazine's content is not just necessary from a readership standpoint either. Industries expand or contract, new businesses start up, and advertising salesmen are always under the gun to produce new revenue. Refreshing a magazine's content often opens up new territory for advertising sales or for new profit centers attached to the basic magazine (directories, card decks, mailing list rentals) so it's certainly in the publication's best interest to keep the magazine informatively entertaining. Fresh writing helps achieve this purpose.

What trade editors need

Since the most basic job of any editor is to provide subscribers with information they want to read, the true "art" of editing is to find and develop information in an interesting, even entertaining, format. In practice, the editor's toughest job is to get to know his particular readers thoroughly enough to be able to predict what they will be interested in.

Most editors quickly come to the conclusion that one size does not fit all. Put another way, a variety of story types is the best way to deliver information. Some readers like news, some like to read about the experiences of others, some like to have just the nuts and bolts they need to perform a task. What becomes one of the most important distinctions for the freelancer is the mix of story types in a trade magazine.

The most important story types include:

News of the field. As we noted in Chapter 1, providing industry news is one of the most important functions for trade magazines. What new product has been developed that will cut costs in production? Which company has found a way to sell windmills in Antarctica? Who's developing a software program that will revolutionize widget design? Why is so and so going out of business? What opportunity has another company taken advantage of that we can too?

The business world's craving for news, and interpretation of news (i.e., Will a new technique render your business obsolete, or will it provide your business an opportunity to be more productive or garner more customers or have a higher profit margin). Does a new president at XYZ Corporation mean that company will be targeting the design/build market, or does it mean they will abandon the design/build market altogether? Will the new wrap-up insurance programs mean that workers compensation will only be for small companies in the future.

News, as one construction industry giant told me, is the lifeblood for making decisions. Trade editors understand this side of the business is one of the most important reasons for a magazine's existence.

How-to and service articles. Service articles are not just a staple in consumer magazines. "The Ten Best Places to Buy a Car" quickly translates into a business equivalent: "The Ten Best Places to Rent a Crane" or "The Five Best Project Management Programs for Commercial Construction."

How-to articles have their place as well, although often trade magazines will concentrate primarily on management how-to, not how-to involving trade, technical or mechanical skills, but there are exceptions to this rule. *The Journal of Light Construction*, for example, will have articles on specific techniques for building foundations, framing roofs, etc. More frequently, however, how-to articles focus on how to do a better job of managing a particular aspect of the business, from accounting to insurance to human resources to risk control.

Experiences. Experience stories include such articles as case histories, project profiles, and company profiles. This kind of story gives the reader a "benchmark" to measure against. In many trade magazines, experience stories are the staple of the feature section because they serve the two most vital purposes of any magazine—informing the reader and providing a *raison d'etre* for advertising.

For a freelancer, experience stories such as these offer a good opportunity both to break into a market and to establish a steady stream of assignments from editors. Most trade editors readily admit that experience stories are a staple in the editorial mix. Readers want to compare what they are doing and how they are doing it against the way it is being done elsewhere. Experience stories are often the most frequently read part of a trade magazine.

Forums. Trade magazines often act as a place where theories or changing conditions can be argued for and against. Legislation, federal, state, and local, almost always affects an industry in one way or another, but more often changing conditions such as rising prices, declining markets, shortages, and changing marketing or management methods are harder for an industry to adjust to than a new piece of law.

The forum aspect of a trade magazine offers opportunity primarily through round-up articles. You can show a trend or survey how industry members are adapting to or leading a change in the conditions of an industry.

Experience stories can also highlight an adaptation of a change and become part of the forum "mix" which can include in-depth interviews with one or more top leaders who are for—or against—the change.

Market information. If you haven't already noticed, market information is the single most prevalent common denominator in trade magazines. Market information, in the broadest sense, includes almost any type of information that will affect an industry, from labor and material supplies to the expansion or changes in the end users of the product, and especially where to sell products and services as well as how to sell them.

This vital part of a trade magazine's mix can be fertile ground for a freelance writer. Readers need to know about new products and techniques. They need to understand where a new market is developing, and where a mature market is beginning to decline. They need to know the new tricks to increase profits; they need to know what old techniques are costing more than they should. They need to know who is buying, who is going to buy in the future, and who is about to stop buying—and why.

Round-up articles, trends, show coverage, service pieces—almost any story type from product reviews to how-tos can be slanted to help build or keep a customer base. For most trade magazine editors, finding and presenting this information is a vital part of their job, so a timely query for articles covering a market are generally given a serious consideration.

Community news may or may not provide a freelancer with ammunition for an assignment. Community news—personnel changes, office moves, awards, changes in operating procedures, and other news that affects day-to-day transactions—is generally gathered through press releases sent by a company or their representative agency. For a freelancer, most of the opportunity in community news comes from working directly with a firm to produce their press releases. Trade freelancers often walk a line between strict freelancing and serving as a one-person public relations agency. While the mechanics of freelancing as a publicist are beyond the scope of this book, it's important to note that many freelancers move into this arena very naturally.

For many, blurring the line between independent freelance journalist and PR flak is anathema. This opinion can be shared by editors as well who will refuse to work with freelance writers who also do public relations work, arguing that such jobs destroy a writer's objectivity. On the other hand, many also deny this argument, pointing out no story is without a bias of some kind and that doing public relations work is an acceptable and financially necessary adjunct to a freelance writing career.

For one thing, the task of writing for a trade magazine forces you to become aware of the industry's players, and in the course of gathering information for an article, it would be very unusual if some relationships didn't develop which led to requests or questions about your ability and willingness to handle some public relations functions.

Whether to handle public relations work as well as freelance journalism is a question all writers must decide individually. But for any writer who covers an industry, it is always worthwhile to note the community news sections of a trade magazine and to remember that as you write more and more about an industry, you become a part of the "community" so those sections also become areas where you can promote your business as well.

Why trade editors need your freelance articles

There are important elements you can bring to a trade magazine that can't be found anywhere else. If you are a beginner in the writing game, you may think I'm being facetious, but as you progress in your career, you'll discover your unique capabilities and perspective are a boon to editors.

Outsourcing. One of the sad realities of the magazine world is that acquisition and downsizing fever has swept it as surely as it has swept the broad spectrum of corporate enterprises. For those who would like to work in magazine publishing, the opportunities have sometimes been limited. For freelancers, however, the downsizing of corporate America has led to increased opportunity for the adept, not just in article opportunities but in a wide range of writing related services.

With downsizing has come a new corporate buzzword: outsourcing. For magazines, both consumer and trade, outsourcing is now a normal function. Magazine schedules tend to be very fluid. If a magazine isn't hitting its "numbers," the revenue expected in its yearly budget, it must often find ways to swell that revenue, sometimes by adding special inserts, sometimes by adding special issues, sometimes by developing new products.

When you must add products, however, in a book that has spent several years reducing its staff to the bare minimum, the editor must look to outside sources to provide material. A boon for the freelancer.

Again, the same situation seems to be holding true for companies within a trade category. Public relations staff becomes overwhelmed and looks for outside help as well, so the more you are known within your industry, the better you can fill in lean times with this type of work as well.

Uniqueness. Beyond the basic essential of needing more material, you are a valuable commodity to editors because you are unique in the *resources* that you have and use.

For a variety of reasons, no two people ever research or write an article exactly the same way for a variety of reasons. You will discover resources that perhaps only you know about or are able to use. One area where this becomes very apparent is with Internet research, which will go into more in a later chapter. So much information is on the Internet that no single person can know, much less find, it all.

People are another resource that will be unique to you. Perhaps, for example, you hit it off with an egotistical CEO who is willing to work with you and no one else. Perhaps your set of resources are deeper in one area than someone else's. A good case in point is my own experience. As an editor for eight years, I have developed a wide range of contacts within the construction industry in Utah, and a usable, but much sparser, range of contacts in the adjoining states. That positions me to be uniquely valuable to magazines who want construction stories from the Rocky Mountain area.

At the same time, I have almost no contacts in the financial industry here, except for those bankers and insurance brokers who specialize almost exclusively in the construction industry. The same holds true for the medical field. I'm familiar to administrative personnel who oversee clinic and hospital construction, but probably invisible to lab managers, doctors and nurses.

Those facts (plus the ability to write coherent sentences) make me uniquely qualified to tackle some stories for the financial and medical fields when the subject is construction, but leave me at sea when it comes to stories on pension fund investment products or biomedical engineering breakthroughs.

I don't want to suggest that you limit your development of resources. Your interests along with your assignments will help determine the resources you cultivate. Truthfully, the more you expand your resources, the more you are willing to push the bounds of your current knowledge, the more valuable you will become.

Freshness. As I've already alluded, editors understand their books need to be refreshed to keep readers reading. One of the simplest ways is to use a variety of writers who style and voice offer some variety.

One of the most undeserved assumptions that many have about trade magazine journalism is that it is "hack writing," permitting rote story information and structure. The story is always the same, only the names change.

At some time in the history of trade magazines that notion may have carried an element of truth. In today's market, however, a consistent diet of well worn stories would kill a magazine of any kind in a relatively short time.

Trade magazines are no different from their counterparts in the consumer press. Editors look for style and freshness as well as substance, and in many ways, writing a trade story that is both informative and lively is even more of a challenge than performing the same feat for a mainstream publication. If getting and holding the attention of an audience who wants to be entertained is crucial, imagine how much more crucial it is for an audience whose members are generally very busy and quite willing to pass by an article with no benefit in its opening.

Saving time and money. I've already talked about how outsourcing has become a way of life in corporate environments, including those in the magazine world. Even without the strain imposed on minimal staff, using freelancers has always been a strategy for magazines because such use saves editors time and money in other ways.

Take a magazine such as *Engineering News-Record* which maintains a group of correspondents as well as a home office staff of editors in charge of certain sectors of construction industry oversight. This magazine still uses some freelance stories even though it has a staff adequate to write the majority of the copy used. Even with a large staff, though, you can't always have the people in place where the story is breaking. And sending a correspondent or staff editor to the site may involve an unacceptable delay. Thus the freelancer saves the magazine time in such a case.

And money as well. When you have to send a staff member, you have to pay for all the attendant travel expenses, and you also add a cost that is difficult to account for on a budget, the cost of not having that staff member available in the main office to maintain their regular duties.

Very often, the expense of paying for a freelance article is less than what the accumulated travel cost would be for a staff member to do a story. Even when a magazine picks up the tab for the freelancer's travel, it is still saving money in the lost office production of the staff member that would have had to go.

The back-up plan. Many, if not all, trade magazine staffs are truly pushing the envelope in terms of productivity. It's common for editors to take work home over the weekend. It's common for editors to average much more than an eight-hour day. It's common for even the best self-managing editors to have a hard time finding a time they can take their accrued vacation.

What happens to a magazine already straining from a work overload when a key editor gets sick or injured or in some way or another cannot work? They had better have a back-up, and in many cases, that's when they will look to regular contributors to the publication for help. An even more common situation is for the lone editor of a small magazine to quit and the publisher is unable to replace the editor in time for the next issue.

The best secret. The best kept secret in writing isn't really much of a secret. Of the approximately 6,000 to 7,000 trade magazines covering business in the U.S., only about 200 are listed in *Writer's Market,* less than half a percent. No wonder beginning writers never think much about them. And of the ones listed that I have seen in the magazine, many are not break-in markets.

I don't mean to criticize *Writer's Market* unreasonably. Like any publication, their first duty is to their primary readers, and those readers generally are most interested in the consumer publications, not trade magazines.

I think there are two reasons why so little information is generally available to writers about trade publications. First and foremost, few universities ever offer a course in trade journalism, much less have it as a focus within the journalism department. Every curricula I've ever seen, with the notable exception of the Medill School of Journalism at Northwestern University, focuses primarily on just two types of periodicals, newspapers and consumer-oriented magazines.

The approach isn't necessarily wrong—good writing technique is much the same in both, as well as in trade magazines. What is astonishing enough is that every year a large number of journalism graduates throughout the country find themselves in the world of the trade magazines without the additional skills they could easily have developed while they were still in school.

Naturally enough, since trade writing receives no emphasis in many departments, an inherent bias develops. Writing for trade magazines isn't true journalism at all — since it isn't taught, it must be merely hacking.

From that thought it's a simple step to the conclusion: "Real" writers don't write for trade magazines; they write for newspapers, consumer magazines, sometimes newsletters, and of course, when they have enough material, book publishers. The other possibility, of course, is to write for ad agencies or public relations firms and departments. I'll bet that very few graduates are ever exposed to the possibilities of working or writing for trade magazines.

Actually, this situation doesn't sadden me much and

shouldn't bother you at all. It certainly cuts down the amount of competition to fight through to get the editor's attention, and from a freelance point of view, that's a useful thing.

On the other hand, a little competition is good as well. It keeps your marketing focused and your writing sharp. Hopefully you will understand by the time you read the rest of this book that writing for trade magazines is anything but hack writing. In many ways it is the most demanding in terms of interviewing and selecting the right facts, quotes, and support materials.

My personal belief is that writing for trade magazines is most closely allied to writing about science. You need to maintain the same high level of credibility and the same faculties of logic and reason which go into good science writing. You must be accurate with both facts and quotations. You must be able to take difficult concepts, explain them succinctly, and explain why they are important to the reader. In some fields, notably medicine and computers, the science writing and trade writing overlap to a large degree because it is hard to understand how to write about the business of medicine without understanding the science, and the same is true to an large extent with the computer hardware and software industries.

More than anything else, you need to bring a keen sense of curiosity to the field of trade writing. What seems on the surface banal and mundane often is intensely fascinating when you break through the outer skin of appearance. There is drama in business. There is passion. There are good guys and bad guys. There are forces of nature to overcome, and forces of nature to maintain. There is honor and heroism; there is greed and deception. There is self-sacrifice; there is self aggrandizement. There is fear; there is courage. Wherever human beings gather, there is a story, and that is just as true in the pages of *Restaurant Business* and *Plastics Technology* as it is in *Family Circle, People, Cosmo,* or any other magazine you care to name. Your writing career, your quest to tell a story about what makes the world tick, is what *you* make of it.

Chapter 3

How to come up with the right idea, pitch it to the right person, and get the assignment.

Assess yourself first.

Coming up with ideas to write about is relatively easy. More difficult is coming up with ideas that will take advantage of your strengths, interest the target magazine's editor, and compel the reader to read. Before we jump in to the basics of developing ideas for trade magazines, understand that the most necessary part of the process is to assess yourself first in terms of your own goals and your current resources.

Everyone reading this book will have a different goal. Some of you want to make a little extra income by moonlighting. Some of you want to improve your professional reputation and career marketability by promoting yourself through writing about your industry. Some of you are writers already, either full or part time, who want to expand your potential income.

The goals portion of this self-assessment should be very

concrete. I'm not talking about: I want to be a dynamic leader who doubles income every year. Be very specific: How many stories do you want to write in how many hours over a given time frame? If you want to write a dozen stories per year, your approach and attitude is going to be different from wanting— perhaps needing—to write three to four stories per week.

Naturally, you probably have in the back of your mind some kind of income figure based on the amount of work you perceive is possible. If you are a veteran writer, you already know that in the writing profession, pay is not linked to time spent. If you are a beginner, you will learn this sometimes unfortunate, sometimes happy fact soon enough.

The most valuable resource you need to assess is the amount of time you can spend working at trade writing. I can't speak for everyone, but I know that roughly for every hour I spend actually writing a trade story, I spend four to six doing research, both for the story itself and to market the story. You need to keep in mind, especially if you are moonlighting, that interviewees can't always be reached on your schedule. Libraries won't always have what you need. The internet can be tied up, or you may be using the wrong search engine to find the right background material easily.

In fact, I would say the largest application of Murphy's Law in writing is that every story will take *only* twice as long as you think it will—if you are very, very lucky.

Other resources need to concern you as well. A good library close at hand is indispensible, but even a good library will seldom—if ever—carry the trade magazines you need to see. More on that in a moment.

Your personal assessment should naturally consider *what* you already know, as well as what you would like to know. You are already in one profession or another, so you have a handle on at least one industrial trade category. If you are a working writer, for instance, then you are already in the publishing industry. Knowing that you know *something* is a start. What other industries either serve your industry or supply it? That's the next logical resource. What industries does your industry serve? What are you curious about in these two areas. What would you like to learn more about?

In a sense, trade writing is a chance to send yourself back to college, only this time, you get to set most of the curricula, you get to interview the "professors," and you get to go at your own pace as long as you meet the deadline.

The other most important resource to assess is *who* you already know. Did you sit at a luncheon with the head of the university's economics department? Do you know every graphic artist in the neighboring division's design department? Do you play pickup basketball against a project manager from the city's largest construction firm? What does your wife's best friend's husband do?

Folks who have writing experience and have been published will understand what I am about to say, and those of you who are just starting out should heed this warning well. There are very few walks on the beach with pensive brow in the daily life of a writer. In terms of the daily grind, the closest vocation I can find is sales.

The reason is, for all magazine writing be it trade or consumer, business revolves around contacts: Interviewing people, meeting people, persuading people, cajoling people, listening to people, commiserating with people, admonishing people, acknowledging people, finding people, keeping in touch with people, networking with people, influencing people, being influenced by people. If you think you can hide in an ivory tower and write for trade magazines, consumer magazines, newspapers, or large book publishers, fiction or non-fiction, you are dead wrong.

Now is the time to assess whether you can become comfortable working with people. Now is the time to assess whether you are willing to overcome your shyness, or your reticence to speak, or your inherited biases against classes of people. Get over it! Ninety-five percent of the people you talk to or work with won't bite, and the other five percent can be gone around! The only way you can get to where you want to go, though, is with the help of a variety of people. And they will sometimes expect help in return.

The first place you are going to need people is in finding markets. A "market," in my definition, means an individual magazine that may be a potential place to sell your writing. A magazine you read for fun but never have any intention of writing for is not a market. A market "category" means all the potential magazines that compete for generally the same readers and, therefore, generally the same advertisers.

Network for magazine copies

Here's where people come into play right off the bat. As I mentioned a few words ago, libraries, even good university libraries, seldom contain enough trade magazines to help you very much. In my main area of expertise, construction and architectural design, I can find about twelve of the five hundred plus magazines in the construction field carried at the state university's library.

Almost every book I've ever read on freelance writing suggests you must read at least six back issues of a particular market before you try query that market. Sage advice, but difficult to follow in the trade magazine world because those back copies simply aren't as available as, say, *Glamour* or *Inc.*, or *Handyman.* If you can't find back copies at the library, or current copies on a magazine rack, the only other place you can go is to someone who subscribes to the magazine.

Actually, having to approach a subscriber to look at back issues isn't as difficult as it might appear. The first place you go, of course, is to friends and close acquaintances who might be in a field you would like to cover. If your neighbor is a baker, for instance, he might subscribe *Modern Baker*, a feature magazine for retail bakers that focuses on production techniques. In fact, he may also subscribe to *Bakery Production and Marketing*, and if his position requires him to do the buying as well, he might read *Milling & Baking News.*

Chances are he will part with a few back issues, or at least let you borrow them for awhile. You can't escape it—if you want to write consistently for trade magazines, you must develop your own library. One exception. If you work for a company that maintains a corporate library, that's a natural place to look for magazines, especially those in your current profession. The drawback, I've found, is that corporate libraries are most often set up to accommodate the top people in the company, are located at headquarters, and if you are out in a branch office or away from the library site, you may see long lag times in ordering materials.

Finding market information in the library.

Libraries can be helpful in finding market information, if not providing copies of the magazines themselves. The first place to start is *Writer's Market*, an annual directory which lists first and foremost the top consumer markets, but also pays some attention to the trade magazine field. What you find in the trade magazine section is generally the tip of the tip of the tip of the iceberg, but it is a good place to start and gives you an idea of the range of fields if not the depth.

Without a doubt the best place to locate addresses for most of the national trade magazines is Standard Rate and Data Service's Volume II, sometimes known as *Business Rate & Data*, *and Business Publication Advertising Source Part 2*, generally titled *Medical Economics*. The Standard Rate and Data Service, SRDS for short, is a directory "bible" used by advertising firms to figure out potential ad costs and campaigns. The primary information it carries is advertising rates for trade magazines, but it will also have a fairly complete address, phone and fax numbers, and a general summary of the magazine's focus. The description also carries an editorial contact, but usually this is usually the editor in chief or the editor. For your needs, however, you must find the managing editor or articles/feature editor which means giving the magazine a call. Queries that go to an editor-in-chief usually go into a trash bin.

One problem with the SRDS is that it has become very expensive, so fewer libraries are carrying it. Ten years ago I could find it in the county library and the city library in Salt Lake, but now only the University of Utah library carries it in this area. Again, if you have an acquaintance in the advertising field, they may have a copy that you could look over.

SRDS is not the only source, however. Oxbridge Communications publishes the *Standard Periodicals Directory* which often lists the managing editor's name as well as the address of the magazine. It's divided into subject categories which makes it easy to research potential markets for a particular focus. The drawback, however, is that other publications, such as directories and newsletters, are part of the listings. The directories are easy to spot, though, and with practice so are the newsletters. Having the addresses of the newsletters can be helpful for researching a topic, but my experience so far is that only a few of the ones you find in this directory use any freelance material.

When you are literally feeling on top of the world about a story idea, you should also check out *Uhlrich's Directory of International Publications*. Uhlrich's Directory will point you toward foreign markets, many of which are published in English. Fortunately, many non-English publications are willing to translate a good article as well, so there is a growing resale market outside of the U.S. More on this topic in Chapter 13.

Three other directories you should be aware of are *Working Press of the Nation, Gebbie's Directory*, and *Bacon's Publicity Checker* which is a very good source for finding out information about magazines. The trouble for those of us who are essentially Scottish when it comes to money is that ordering your own copy of *Bacon's* or *Gebbie's* is very expensive. By the same token, updated versions are not as common a reference in libraries as they used to be, and when I've found one in local libraries, the copy they have is almost always two or more years out of date which is much too long.

I run into the same problem with *Working Press* which is a directory built around newspaper editors as well as magazines. Whenever I find a copy in the library, it's just too old. Still, your library may have a better budget or these publications may be given higher priority than the *Standard Periodical Directory* which seems to be what most systems use in the Salt Lake City area.

If there is a good magazine or newsletter for updating trade magazine markets, I haven't found it. *Writer's Digest*, a magazine dedicated to freelance writers of all ilks, carries a section on new markets each month. Occasionally a trade publication will find its way onto these pages, but if you are going to subscribe, do so with the understanding that you will get a ton of useful information about almost every kind of writing except for trade magazines.

Another source that does a somewhat better job is a newsletter called *Writing For Money* published by the Blue Dolphin Press. Again, the focus is primarily on the consumer markets, not trade magazines, but new trade magazines are listed when the publication hears about them. One problem with this publication, however, is that the publisher is always experimenting with the format, so I have found consistency in receiving my issues to be a problem. In their defense, they have always responded promptly to a phone call, but you get tired of making that call every other issue.

On the Internet, the best source to point you to the major publishers is *Gebbie's Directory*. I found it using the Yahoo search engine's Business: Trade Magazines page which will also show you some others not listed under the major publishers in Gebbie's. With the publication of this book, Dixon-Price Publishing has set up a directory of both major trade magazine publishers and a directory by industry of individual magazine sites.

Coming up with ideas

For some writers, coming up with ideas to write about is the easiest part of the writing task; for others, the most difficult. To be honest, I can generate enough ideas in a day to keep me busy writing for a decade. I believe the same is true for most professional writers, and how to do it is no great secret: Make lists.

Analyze. What kinds of lists? The answer will vary from individual to individual, and to an extent from industry to industry. Across the board, however, I advise you first to make a list of your own interests and questions you would like answered. As you make contacts within an industry, keep a second list of the interests and the questions your contacts would like answered.

The third list you should probably make on a continuing basis is a list of current trends, needs, and interests that society as a whole seems to be developing. Where do you come up with this information? Start with your daily newspaper. I like to cull through the newspaper for trend ideas, particularly through articles that have a local byline from either the paper's staff or from a freelancer. I don't rule out articles that have a national tag such as AP or Knight-Ridder, but I make that a separate list which I loosely label "Already Identified Trends."

Actually, there are always two kinds of trends: national trends and local trends. National trends, though, almost always start out as a local trend. By keeping your eyes open, you can often get a jump on the national news services.

Categorize. So far, this list keeping advice sounds fairly general, something you could use to generate ideas for consumer publications—and so you can. But as a trade writer, you have other lists to generate. For each industry you cover, as I noted above, you need to keep a list of what interests your contacts and what questions they may have. The second industry list you need is a list of what they are doing.

In my main field, commercial construction and design, I keep a running list of projects that are underway and a tickler file of completion dates for those projects I believe will be the most interesting to write about. At the same time, I keep a lists of the trends and innovations in the construction industry, and the interests and questions of my contacts in the industry.

Synthesize. When it's time to come up with story ideas, I lay the three lists out in front of me and start putting categories together like the old Chinese food menus:

• one from column A (project) and one from column B (trend)—"Utah's First Design/build Public Project";

• or one from A and one from C (project and contact question)—"Will Pre-qualified Mod Rates Keep Construction Costs Down on Kennecott's New Smelter?"

- or one from B and one from C—"Is design/build driving the trend to owner-controlled insurance programs?";
- or even two together from A, B, or C—"A Tale of Two Hotels"; "Staffing Is Different for Design/build and Hard Bid"; and "'Green Builders Eye Soy [Oil] Futures."

Think of developing a topic as simply like a game of pick up sticks. Throw the elements in the air and pick up the first two that land. I recall that comedy writer Gene Perret uses this basic method in developing jokes and coming up with skit ideas. Because of the way our mind works, this synthesis of one idea with another takes place even when we aren't conscious of doing it. Whether consciously or unconsciously, we are always making comparisons and contrasts. This procedure is just a formalized way to get that analytical equipment working.

But there is more work to do. A topic, regardless of how intellectually intriguing, is not yet an article idea. The next step is to take a particular slant on that broad topic.

A slant is nothing more than a particular and specific roadmap that tells your reader (and editor) what you are going to be talking about, why you are going to be talking about it, and how you are going to be talking about it.

In my college days, we called this approach the thesis, and we were taught to write a thesis sentence using a very convenient structure. The main clause was always joined to a subordinate clause beginning with "because." When you actually write your query or article, you rework this thesis sentence to suit the language of the market. Start off with the form, however, and generally you can think of it as a single sentence summary of your article.

Using a topic from the list above:

Utah is contracting the Scott Matheson Courthouse as it's first design/build project [main clause] *because the state hopes to get a building* [primary subordinate] *that costs less than comparable courthouses, uses less public staff to administer the project, and can be erected faster than by waiting for the design to be finished to*

49

build the project under the old design/bid/build method [secondary subordinate clauses].

Whew, that's much too long a sentence to use as a lead, but it doesn't matter. In fact, what I did with the sentence was break it up into three or four sentences that made up my "billboard paragraph" when I wrote the article. But this is the thesis sentence I built from.

Notice how neatly this sentence structure does the work for you. The main clause tells you what the article will be about. The "because" tells you the why, and then the three clauses subordinated to the "because" basically sets up a three-section structure, a "how" for your story.

Let me clue you in on a little secret that journalism schools often understate: There is no such thing as an unbiased story. Everything you write—everything—from travel articles to poems to elegies to "hard news" stories—every nonfiction article is an *argument*. You are persuading your reader to your point of view regardless of how detached, unemotional, and Jack Webb ("Just the facts, ma'am) you try to be. And because you are arguing, because you are persuading your reader, through the facts you are giving him and the way those facts are presented, this "thesis sentence" structure will work over and over and over again.

Oh yeah? What about the second topic you wrote earlier? Well, you have to answer the question the topic poses, so the thesis sentence becomes the answer:

Will Pre-qualified Mod Rates Keep Construction Costs Down on Kennecott's New Smelter?

Your positive answering thesis might be: Using mod rates to pre-qualify contractors will keep construction costs down on Kennecott's new smelter [main clause/assertion] because contractors with low mod rates generally can bid lower, are generally better at managing projects, and are better at managing safety which is what causes costs overruns on many industrial projects [primary and secondary clauses].

Or negative: Using mod rates to pre-qualify contractors won't keep construction costs down on the Kennecott smelter project because mod rates only indicate past safety performance, not craft quality, and are no guarantee of future safety performance that holds down workers compensation costs.

A caveat. The thesis sentence structure is primarily for your use. It's a mechanical tool to provoke you into thinking about how to slant your article. It asks you to take a stand. It asks you how you will organize the information and because you must organize the information, what the nature of that information will be. It asks you to assume an attitude as well. In the two examples above, the attitude of the thesis sentence was serious, thoughtful, showed an insider's understanding of how the construction industry works, and radiated confidence that the reader would understand the basics as well.

Would these two examples make good reading in an article? Maybe in a longer essay such as journals use, but not in a fast-paced trade magazine article that must hold the reader's attention. Use the thesis as a starting point, then break it down into modules with a faster pace. This procedure gives you a slant that you can pitch.

Take the smelter thesis for example: "Kennecott Corp. plans to save money on its smelter project by using safer contractors who can generally deliver projects at a lower overall cost," or "By pre-qualifying only contractors with top safety records, Kennecott Corp. bets it can keep construction costs down on its new smelter."

Consider the type of article. Although the thesis sentence approach works for most articles, you must also consider what type of article you are writing and work the thesis pattern to fit the type. The difference is usually one of substance, not form. For a show article, which will not have the same aggressive argumentation as our smelter article might, your thesis tone will not be as strong: The annual World of Concrete provided attendees with a glimpse of the future because the largest construction equipment firms unveiled new machines controlled by computers. Or maybe: The annual World of Concrete was sparsely attended because equipment and material suppliers have been too busy fending off labor strikes to concentrate on developing new products this past year.

While I wouldn't use either of these theses as my topic sentence in the lead, I would use them to help me define my subject for an editor.

Topic -spoking. In his book *How to Sell 75% of Your Freelance Writing,* Gordon Burgett develops the notion of topic-spoking. Most freelancers who make a full-time living use this technique although they may call it by a different name. The basic tenet of topic spoking is that you have done a body of preliminary research, and to maximize your earnings from that research, your goal should be to reuse that research in as many different articles as possible. To accomplish that task, however, you have to come up with more than one slant, more than one possible thesis to develop from the body of research. Put simply: Research once, sell often.

In my opinion, trade magazines are almost perfect for this approach to marketing articles because the overlap in readership is much less than in consumer magazines.

Take the manufacture of any material object from a glass marble to a 40-story office building. With any type of production, there are always several good business stories to tell:

• How was it manufactured? (a case history; a how-to manufacture, a profile of the manufacturer, a story

• How was it developed? (a case history of how you develop such a product; a profile of the man or the team that developed it; a how-to on forming a team to develop such a product; news that it has been developed or is being developed; a trend story that it shows a trend toward this product, or that it is bucking the trend away from this kind of product; an issue story on how or why the product's development could lead to difficult legislative, social, or business consequences.)

• Why was it developed? (The trend story here focuses on

why; the how-to stories available can target a variety of potential ways to market the product because it was developed for a customer; the profile can focus on the company's overall goal, or on an individual or team's goal.)

• Who was it developed for? (What's the customer trend? How will customers use the product? How will the manufacturer market the product? How advertise? How sell? How distribute? What do competitive products do? What are all the products in the category? What kind of competitive edge does the product give the manufacturer? The customer?)

Let's use the Kennecott smelter as an example:

• How was it manufactured? An on-site story about the construction of the smelter. A profile story on the project's general contractor who is building its first smelter. A profile story on the brick maker who made the refractory lining for the smelter. A profile story on the foundation contractor who had to build a uniquely difficult mat foundation.

• How was it developed? A case history story of how the design team sought to eliminate problems in previous smelters. Our story on how the pre-qualification of contractors led to a lower cost project than originally anticipated. A story on how the structural engineer approached the design of this one-of-a-kind foundation. A round-up story on the innovations in smelter design over the past 20 years. A trend story about how computer control is changing the nature of designing a smelter. A trend story about how workers compensation insurance costs are affecting the award of the general contract on all large projects such as smelter. A trend story on how owners are beginning to use owner-controlled-insurance-programs (OCIPs) and why self-insuring means they will only use contractors with an outstanding safety record.

• Why was it developed? A trend story on how the mining industry is reducing smelter costs to stay competitive in a global market. A round-up story on how U.S. smelters are becoming too old to remain competitive. A round-up story on how environmental regulations are driving smelters to modernize. A profile story on how Kennecott has discovered that systematic environmental upgrades to facilities has paid off in lower operating costs.

• Who was it developed for? A trend story on how the domestic market for copper is up or down. A trend story on the growing global market for copper. A round-up story about the doubtful—or delightful—future for ore refiners who can maintain production while cutting costs. A trend story about the pinch in spot markets for copper. A trend story about how specialty metal fabricators are using more copper. A profile of a copper exporter. A round-up on how communities are developing tax credits for encouraging refineries to use cleaner technologies.

Now I have twenty-plus story possibilities to pitch to a variety of markets, and in each case I can use the research that I put into the story on contractor selection, especially the contacts I've made at Kennecott and with their in-house design engineer, as a starting point to develop any one of the other stories. Could we come up with more? Sure. Just make a list of items, cut them up, throw them in a hat and draw out two at a time. Some of the juxtapositions won't make any sense, but some will be viable story ideas, and even more important, will jog new ideas in your head.

What does the reader want?

If the approach to coming up with an idea seems a bit mechanical, it is. Before you fire off a query to the closest trade editor, you still need to do some homework.

Coming up with ideas using the preceeding method is basically for your benefit. But ultimately, the story won't worth a dime to an editor if it doesn't fit into the universe of what the reader is interested in.

This is a tricky area for trade writers for a very good reason. We are both *in* the industry—and not in the industry. We can easily determine what an average Joe would want to read about, but not the average Joe in the audience we are writing for, and that's one of the elements of writing for trade magazines which makes it such a challenging and rewarding profession.

Back to our Kennecott example. Unless you are an engineer or an architect, can you tell anything at all about the difference between one smelter smoke stack and another other than the general shape and height? Probably not. Me either. But the differences, while seldom profound, are important to the manufacturer because those differences very likely affect his ability to be profitable.

To know whether your story is going to have any interest for a reader in the target industry, you are going to have to develop a network of industry "mentors" who can give you a good sense of what's interesting and what isn't within an industry.

As a rookie trade writer, I was approached by salesman who had a great story about how flyash was being used in a new product, a flowable concrete "fill" that could be back-filled into utility trenches to keep them more stable. Never having heard of such a thing, I thought it might be the greatest story since Maris hit 61 homers. Trenches and the utility piping suffer major damage from the ground shifting too much or from a load being applied overhead, such as a truck running over the uncompacted fill.

Before I jaunted off to pen the story, however, I checked with a concrete industry guru about whether this was a story worth doing. Talk about deflated! This "new" product had been around for about two decades; everybody in the industry not only knew about it, but also knew that it was too expensive for most common applications. "After all," he told me, "There are really only so many things you can do with flyash in concrete, and most of them have been known about since the 30s."

Patrick Clinton suggests in *Writing for the Business Press* that there is a pyramid of information in the business world which writers must learn to use. At the base of the pyramid are the thousands of companies who use a product. Their identities and opinions are known to the salesmen of the product; the salesmen are known by the sales manager; the sales managers are known by the marketing manager; the marketing managers are known to the VP of sales, the marketing managers' association, and in turn, the association is known very often by academics. Clinton suggests that the "handful" of people on the top of the pyramid can give you access to all the information, whether they know it or not, and that by working down the pyramid, you can find the specific details and experiences that give life to a piece.

He also suggests working across multiple pyramids to add depth to a story. For instance, if you are doing a story on the housing boom in Utah, you talk to builders, you talk to the Home Builders Association, and perhaps you talk to construction loan officers. Jumping across the pyramid to the economist at the state university who tracks building permit valuation will give you some additional depth. Jumping to another pyramid and talking to an officer with the state job service will give you additional information, etc.

The mentors you need to develop are both at the top and at the bottom of this pyramid. The ones at the top will give you access to the information you need; the ones at the bottom will tell what stories need to be written today.

Finding the right editor

The best idea in the world with the most intriguing slant ever imagined is going to be pitched into the wastebasket if it goes to the wrong editor. This truism applies to trade magazines just as much as it does to consumer magazines, and for the freelancer, the lack of a frequently updated market directories that focus on who the right contact is—such as *Writer's Market* does—just compounds the difficulty.

During my time with McGraw-Hill, I was at various times an assistant editor, a senior editor, a co-editor, a contributing editor, and a "just plain" editor. During each of these titular iterations, I performed essentially the same job: select the stories, write the stories, copy edit the other editor's stories (when we had another editor), and proof the layout.

Since I've been a freelancer, I've found that my circumstance wasn't particularly unusual. There are generally accepted standards about what an editor does as opposed to what a managing editor does, but the size of the staff really dictates how much the editorial work can compartmentalized. Magazines, much like any other small business enterprise, tend to assign responsibilities to those who have the talent to handle them, regardless of title.

In practice, you will very seldom do just one article for a magazine. The financial reality is that it is in both your best interest and theirs to develop a long-term relationship. You benefit from having a steady pool of assignments; they benefit by having a writer they can depend on to deliver what they need.

The challenge really comes with the initial approach. Who's the right one to pitch an article to? Here, trade magazines often outdo their consumer counterparts in both friendliness and helpfulness.

Your first step will be to look at a magazine's masthead if you have secured a sample copy. Generally the managing editor is the one you want to pitch an article to, unless the masthead tells you their is a *Features* or *Articles* editor.

If none of these titles are listed, but there are multiple editors, I would pitch first to what you determine is the lowest titled editor, perhaps the assistant editor or the associate editor. Even if they are not the editor who assigns articles, they will most likely pass the query on to the right person.

For the most part, I've seen this approach work only with the trade magazines. If you were to take that approach with most consumer magazines, your query would generally go into the trash or straight to a form rejection. Ergo, when you take your research to develop a query for the consumer magazine, you have to make sure you find out whose right for the pitch. With trade magazines, there's usually more leeway.

If the magazine has an editorial assistant, that person can be most helpful. The editorial assistant often routes the mail within the office and will be the one to answer routine inquiries for sample copies, writing guidelines, and such other daily routine matters including screening calls. A quick call to the editorial assistant will usually give you the name of the right editor to pitch and at the same time you can get a sample copy, writing guidelines, if any, and an editorial calendar for the year to help plan your work.

By the way, don't pitch to contributing editors. They are either freelancers like you who have developed a long-term relationship with the magazine, often writing a particular column, or they may be staff members in the main association the magazine is directly affiliated with. The only exception is when an association's contributing editor, whom you personally know, may be open to recommending a piece to the magazine's staff. In general though, I would never approach a contributing editor until you have developed a relationship with the main staff and understand how the contributing editors fit into their scheme.

Refine your idea

You aren't ready to write your query until you can write your lead. We've talked about how to come up with the idea and develop it into a thesis sentence. Before you start to write your query, you must decide if that thesis sentence can stand as your lead or if the thesis sentence must be reworked a bit.

How do you determine whether to rework it? A thesis sentence tells the reader what you are going to write about, and summarizes what information you will give him. A lead must go a step further. It must grab his attention, at least long enough to get him to the thesis sentence.

Every book on writing that I've ever read says much the same thing: If you can't get the editor's attention with the lead, you won't get the reader's. There are many tried and true methods of leading an article, but in trade magazines, the number one "grabber" by far is a reference to money.

It stands to reason that a lead focused on money in some way is the core grabber for a trade. Readers don't go to trade magazines to learn Hatha Yoga or spiritual awareness. The self-improvement they seek is profitability—in their job and in their business, marketability both personally and for their business, cost-effectiveness to improve their promotion potential and to increase company profits. Even such very personal subjects as time management and relationships with co-workers must toe the bottom line: a profit for the individual (if you have more time, you can produce more money, if you can work better with others, you can produce more money through increased effectiveness).

Mo' money is the benefit your lead should stress. That will grab the reader's attention.

Such a lead is implied in our Kennecott thesis sentence: Using mod rates to pre-qualify contractors will keep construction costs down on Kennecott's new smelter because contractors with low mod rates generally can bid lower, are generally better at managing projects, and are better at managing safety which is what causes costs overruns on many industrial projects.

Now, let's go for the throat in our lead paragraph. Make mine money:

Rising labor costs and higher prices for construction materials pale beside the 35 percent increase in medical costs for injured workers in the last two years. (Most businessmen in the mining and construction industries know the medical payout on their workers compensation insurance has boomed. But what does it mean?)

That increase means owners who do business with unsafe contractors—who must pay higher than average workers compensation rates—typically pay 5 to 10 percent more to build their projects. (The reader is mostly hooked at this point. If you are a risk manager who wants to keep his job, or a small business owner who has to build a new building, you understand the bad implications immediately. Just in case they don't, though, spell it out.)

On a $10 million project, that difference can mean up to $1 million extra without an extra million in building value. (This will gag the small business owner; the risk manager, *and* the large company CEO.)

Imagine the potential extra cost to build an $800 million smelter. (Okay, gotcha now. CEO tugging on collar as he imagines explaining $80 million in lost profit to shareholders. Risk manager mentally developing a resume for a different job as he imagines explaining $80 million overrun to CEO. Notice that this sentence is geared to transition right into our Kennecott thesis sentence. Boom. Two paragraph lead—the grabber paragraph and then the thesis paragraph.)

Trade articles won't abide long leads. Trade magazine readers are the ultimate skimmers. The reason they take the magazine in the first place is to keep up to date, to make sure they are keeping their competitive edge. If your lead doesn't show right away there's something in it for them, they're off to the next article. Consequently, a lead of more than a couple of graphs is too much, even on a three or four thousand word article.

How will you prove your "argument?"

You have the lead written, now you must tell the editor how you plan to back up your thesis. You don't need to go into great detail here, just give an overview. Will you interview four or five industry experts? Will you talk to the guys in the field who have to do everyday what you are asserting today? Will you cite private or government statistics to prove what you say is true or to show the trend is in that direction.

What order will the information go in? Again, if you have developed the right thesis, you can easily tell the editor the order of the article. If not, go back to the drawing board until you can.

Think of your article as individual chapters, about five altogether. The first chapter is your lead. The second, third, and fourth chapters, which you will make subheads for, are the body of your article where you will tell the industry's readers why and how and when to use the information you're giving them, or why and how and when the events happened and what they were. The last chapter is your close, a summation of all you've told them.

If you aren't sure just how to make up your chapters, take a look at the articles in the magazine you are planning to pitch to. If you break them down by "chapters", you'll quickly see that subheads are guides to the articles construction, and you will get a sense of how the editor likes to see a story developed.

While you're at it, count the number of sources quoted. How many quotes are from industry members, how many are from non-industry experts, how many are citations from written materials? This exercise also tells you what you will need to provide in terms of expert resources. Most editors have a set of expectations they've developed over the years. Some will want at least three sources; some five; some more. Some will want quotes from at least three industry members along with citations from two or more reference works. If your query reassures them you will use the right number of resources in your article, it helps sell the idea to the editor.

As you are going through this exercise, it's also good to note how the articles are finished off. Does the editor seem to prefer a summation, a closing anecdote, a summary quotation?

Pitching the article

Query letters follow a fairly standard format for the very simple reason that it works well. It's best to use the same lead as you would use in your article to begin your query. The technique really serves two purposes. First, if you've written an interesting lead one that has an element of grabber and an element of organization, it is going to interest the editor. Human nature being what it is, if an editor is interested by a lead, the natural assumption he will make is that the reader will be interested as well.

Second, the good lead also tells the editor you are firmly in control of the article's organization, a situation that can't always be determined in a phone call.

Follow the lead paragraph or two with two or three paragraphs explaining how you will go about researching and what information you will include in the article. Your slant is already in the lead, and the explanation should reinforce your understanding of who the right sources are to interview and your understanding of the important issues to cover.

The last paragraph of your query can be a simple bio of who you are and what experience you bring to this particular article. If you don't have any experience in this kind of article, you shouldn't mention that. Again, the editor should have formed a positive opinion of your potential from the lead and explanatory paragraphs, so there's no point shooting yourself in the foot by saying you've never written an article in your life, and certainly not one about retail sales of refrigerators.

By the way, don't forget to ask for the business in your last sentence. If you need some examples or more information on writing queries, you should take a look at Gordon *Burgett's Writer's Guide to Query Letters and Cover Letters* and John Wood's *How to Write Attention-Grabbing Query & Cover Letters*. There are other books out on the subject, but I've found these two the most succinct yet inspirational.

Is a written query necessary? Not always. But my experience as an editor, and a straw poll I've taken of others, tells me to be wary of a writer new to my experience who has sent me nothing in writing. Even a simple letter gives the editor some idea of your style, your ability to use words, your ability to organize thoughts, and therefore your potential to write a good article.

Emphasize your ability to research and your plan for doing so. Editorial decisions, like most things in life, have shades of gray. I have worked with freelancers who were marginal writers at best, but great researchers. Their articles were easy to fix, so I continued to work with them even knowing their articles would require rewriting and guidance.

The reverse is also true. I have had a couple of experiences with excellent stylists who just couldn't seem to dredge up much in the way of substance, and frequently their stylistic flourishes got in the way of a meaningful story. Here's an editorial secret: Of these two choices, I'll take the first type over the second every time. And I suspect I'm in the majority on this subject.

So send a query letter the first three or four times you

write for a particular magazine. For one thing, it helps you organize the article in your mind. For another, it reinforces your capability with an editor.

Phone queries. At some point, as you develop your relationship with an editor, it's going to be acceptable to both of you to make your pitch on a phone call. What's different about pitching an article by phone, I believe, is that you actually can pitch more than one article at a time and find out almost immediately whether you are going to get the assignment or not.

Do you have to be just as prepared as when you write a query? Well, yes and no. It's always good practice to have a thesis sentence summary in mind, but after working with a magazine long enough, some basic ground rules are understood by both parties. When I pitch an article to *Intermountain Contractor* which I worked with for eight years, or for that matter most of the Dodge Construction Publications, I don't have to list who I intend to research because it's understood through the culture of the publications that project profile articles, their main type of feature, should contain quotes from the contractor's project manager, the architect, an owner's representative, and probably the project superintendent as well as any engineering consultant when that element of work is focused on.

I don't have to tell the Dodge editors exactly who I am going to talk to. In fact, when it is a story outside of my state, they will occasionally tell me who to call. More likely though, I'm going to talk to the contractor first and get a list of names and phones from him. It's the simplest way of learning about these sources, and it's almost a matter of unwritten etiquette for this particular type of article.

Check your status. There's more than one way to freelance to trade magazines, and depending upon the relationship you develop with a particular editor, your work could consist of:

"On-spec" or open assignments. This situation is the most frequent when you are first making contact with a magazine. Although the editor may like your query, he won't commit specifically to pay you for the article until he sees it. Fair enough.

The drawback is that you may spend your time and effort writing an article, and then find the editor doesn't want to use the article after all and therefore won't pay you for your effort.

In my experience, though, trade magazine editors generally will work with a writer to make the article acceptable unless deadline pressure doesn't allow the time needed to fix the piece. This attitude I believe is generally different from consumer magazines where the number of writers to choose from is often enormous so the editor's motivation to work with a writer is somewhat limited. If you study a copy of the trade magazine and then duplicate the basic requirements of number of sources, breakout of chapters, length of lead and overall tone—in short producing a readable article—it is very unlikely that you won't be paid for your work.

The other step you can take to avoid a situation where you won't get paid is to stay away from strictly news or trend articles when you first approach a trade magazine. How-to and profile articles are typically "evergreens" in the trade business, capable of being run in any month, and thus aren't tied in as closely to a particular issue's deadline.

Assignments. Once you have developed a relationship with an editor, he's as likely to call with an assignment as you are to pitch an article. The legal position is different between "on spec" and assignments. When you are writing on spec, the magazine has no obligation to pay you if you don't produce an acceptable article. With an assignment, the magazine does have an obligation to pay something for spending your time and effort.

If your article isn't acceptable for reasons beyond your control, such as a change in the editorial calendar or a last minute change in the magazine's focus for the target issue, you are entitled to a "kill" fee. Sometimes other situations crop up—you're not able to make connection with the sources the editor wants interviewed, you're not able to prove the thesis he wants proved or find the information that needs to be found in time for the article to make deadline. Kill fees, however, never ever cover the cost of your time. The best way to protect yourself is to stay in communication with the editor during the course of the article to make sure you are on track and that the assignment is still viable.

When an article has been assigned, the publication is responsible for the expenses you incur in producing the article, including any travel expenses. When you are writing on spec, theoretically you should be reimbursed for expenses when the article is accepted. If it's not accepted, you will be out any money you spent for travel, phone calls and the like, so take care before you go ahead with a spec article that is going to cost very much to produce. It's much better to scrounge your neighborhood for articles to pitch to a new magazine than to come up with a brilliant idea which you must hop on a plane to follow through on.

Stringing. Stringing is a common practice in newspaper work, and it can be productive for you in a few ways. As a stringer, you can pitch stories, or simply pitch an idea for a story that the staff will write and be paid a "finder's fee." You may be given specific assignments on a regular basis. Sometimes stringers are asked to perform research for staff. For awhile I was a stringer for an aviation publication. I never wrote a word for the magazine, but because two large aerospace firms are headquartered nearby, I was asked to do such things as pick up court documents, find phone numbers and contacts, and send clippings from the local newspaper about these two firms.

Stringing can often take on a more focused assignment and a contractual agreement. Often the "contributing editors" you see are "stringers" for a particular aspect of an industry, producing a periodic column, and keeping the home staff up to date on any important developments in that field. Some magazines come up with contractual agreements that spell out what's expected on both sides. I know of several magazines who have contractual agreements with their "correspondents."

In those cases where a contractual agreement is arranged, the magazine will often require the correspondent to write solely for them, and if the correspondent wants to continue freelancing, he or she must generally agree to do so only outside the magazines target industry. A correspondent contract has the benefit of reliable paychecks and sometimes even other benefits such as a healthplan or participation in a 401(k), but seldom does a correspondent contract pay enough to live on, so you must weigh the advantage of the benefit against what you may be giving up by not writing for a variety of magazines in your field.

There are no guarantees that you won't get stiffed one or more times during your career. In fact, the chances are good that you will. You can minimize your chances of being burned by making sure you produce the article that you agreed to produce and that the editor expects.

Be most cautious with magazines who are not part of a national or regional publishing company. There are many perfectly legitimate locally owned magazines with great reputations, but most trade writers I know who have been stiffed have lost their money at the hands of a local start-up. At the same time, my most consistent customer and the one who pays the quickest is a small trade publishing company that covers just two western states. *Caveat escritore.*

Chapter 4

Getting Acquainted with the Major Trade Magazine Publishers

Most readers will already be acquainted with one or more trade magazines, and that's all to the good. What this chapter will do is give you just the briefest glimpse into the world of trade magazine publishers, focusing primarily on the largest conglomerates.

Like many other segments of business, trade magazine publishing has undergone a tremendous amount of activity in mergers and acquisitions. One company in particular, Primedia, has aggressively moved to the forefront in the trade magazine world during the 1990s. When they haven't pursued an acquisition, they have pursued other beneficial business ties, often with some interesting joint operations or mutual ties. By the time I finish typing this chapter, for instance, I suspect they will have closed yet another deal.

Primedia has grown from a company known as K-3. The company works on what I consider a great premise which they proclaim on the home page of their web site: "For every person, there's at least one special interest. For every interest, there's a desire for information."

If that isn't the heart of modern magazine publishing, I don't know what is. Altogether, Primedia publishes 222 magazine titles, 220 consumer and business information products, such as new home guides and apartment guides, owns 47 trade shows and has more than 175 web sites. In 1998, sales were about $1.5 billion and there were about 7,000 employees. Not bad for a company founded in 1989 which didn't even have its Initial Public Offering until 1995.

One magazine published by a Primedia subsidiary is *Folio*, the magazine of magazines. You'll be surprised at how many consumer publications you see in the local grocery store are produced by Primedia. There is no particular guiding light other than "people with a special interest" so they produce books as diverse as *New York, American Baby, Seventeen,* and *Soap Opera Digest.* They have an entire group targeting just youth with such mags as *Teen Beat, Tiger Beat* and *16 Magazine.*

When you get to specialty publications—which are often on the border between consumer and trade publications— Primedia's Special Interest Publications Group and its McMullen Argus Publishing subsidiary put out such well known "niche" magazines as *Cats, Horticulture, Lowrider Magazine, Mustang Illustrated, Street Rodder, Surfing, Truckin', Volleyball, Crafts Magazine, McCall's Quilting, Shutterbug, Southwest Art, Nautical World, Horse & Rider, Equus, County Journal, Vegetarian Times, American History, British History, Early American Homes, Bowhunter, Fly Fisherman Magazine, Pro Football Weekly, Sail,* and my personal favorite, *VW Trends.* And folks, I have barely scratched the surface with this list.

More to the point about the importance of trade magazine publishing. Primedia's first acquisition in 1989 was to acquire the technical and trade publisher Intertec which was first begun in 1886. Along with this acquisition, the company also acquired the Macmillan Book Clubs, renamed as Newbridge Communications, and voila, the Specialty Media and Education groups were in business. For trade and business writers, Intertec is a very important subsidiary. It publishes about 100 trade magazines and newsletters, and its book publishing arm has more than 350 books in print.

The company proves that it is possible to get synergy through trade magazine publishing because they publish in several industries: Ten publications are dedicated to Agriculture; Automotive, and Trucking, 11; Communications and Entertainment, 17; Electrical, 5; Municipal, 5; Health & Fitness, 2; Real Estate & Investing, 5; Mining and Construction, 11; Printing and Packaging, 4; Apparel & Textiles, 4; Facilities Management, 3; and Marketing and Publishing, 10, including *Folio*, the magazine about the magazine industry. It makes sense that Primedia would publish *Folio* because one of its other products is *Bacon's Directory* which is an essential list of publishing industry and other media contacts.

But Primedia's situation, and Intertec's in particular, is instructive. With the demise of general interest magazines that began in the late 1950s, major magazine publishers have increasing pointed to readers with a "special interest" who want specialized information. Although specialized, many of Intertec's titles have more than 100,000 subscribers which is an amazing number for a trade magazine. At the same time, they also have profitable magazines with less than 20,000 subscribers.

The range of Intertec's publications cuts across so many industries that you could call them a "horizontal" trade publisher. But there are other publishers who do just fine with a "vertical" approach.

McGraw-Hill is one publisher who does very, very well with a vertical approach. McGraw-Hill's big moneymaker, of course, is *Business Week*. Begun more than 100 years ago, *Business Week* is not what I would define as a "trade" publication but a general interest publication about business and finance. In that sense its competitors include such magazines as *Fortune*, *Barron's*, some of the Crain newspaper chain, the Business Journal newspapers as well as the *Wall Street Journal*.

When a magazine reports on news across several industries, it is part of the "business press." In this category. In addition to the publications mentioned in the previous paragraph, the business press can include the business section of most daily papers and many independent newspapers and magazines that report on local, regional, or national news across a spectrum of industries. A true "trade magazine" reports specifically on a single industry. It may report some general business news, but almost always that general news will have an impact on the magazine's particular industry.

McGraw-Hill used to be broader in its approach to trade magazines, but it sold several off in the 1980s and consolidated its trade magazine efforts in two major industries, construction and aerospace. In construction, it publishes two of the most prestigious books covering the two broadest divisions of the construction industry. *Architectural Record*, which became the official publication of the American Institute of Architects two years ago, concentrates on the practice of commercial and high-end residential architecture. *Engineering News-Record* follows the news of actual construction in the industry—buildings, highways, utilities, you name it. They are among the most respected magazines in the construction industry.

Beginning in the 1980s, McGraw-Hill began acquiring a network of regional construction magazines under their Dodge Division which reports about new construction projects much like the *Commerce Daily* reports about government procurement needs. These publications, known as the Dodge Construction Publications, have a dominant position in many of the regions they serve with titles such as *Intermountain Contractor*, celebrating its fiftieth anniversary, the *Denver Daily Journal*, *The Green Sheet* in Los Angeles, *Daily Pacific Builder* in San Francisco, *Louisiana Contractor*, *New York Construction News* and more. These magazines are an example of how regional publications serving an industry can build an audience that values them more than many national publications.

McGraw-Hill's other prime trade publication is *Aviation Week & Space Technology*. This dean of all things aviation is supported by a variety of specialized trade newsletters such as *Aviation Daily*, *Aerospace Daily*, *The Weekly of Business Aviation*,

70

Airports, ATC Market Report, Aero Safety & Maintenance and *Inside Aviation/Aerospace IT* known in the industry as *Inside It.* So well respected is this information source that its web site boasts 600,000 visitors per month. If you are in any kind of aviation management, *Aviation Week* publications are must reads.

While I must save a discussion of even all of the major trade magazine publishers for another book, there are some companies who are a must to know about, even when you don't think you will be writing for the industries they cover.

Cahners Business Information is another horizontal publisher whose list of publications is so long that it is difficult to think of an industry where they don't have at least one publication and often more. I counted more than 130 magazines on a recent search, including such well known titles as *Variety* and *Publisher's Weekly*, which are among the trade magazines that have developed a popular following as well. Within their industries, however, such magazines as *Lasers & Optronics, Library Journal*, and *Interior Design* are read with a fervor usually reserved for the *New York Times*.

That's the good news. The bad news, and this applies to almost every horizontal publisher I've dealt with, is that there is almost no consistency in pay or frequency for using freelance writers between the publications. As a freelancer, if you write for *Building Design and Construction*, you likely will make less but be paid faster than if you write for *Professional Remodeler*.

Another horizontal giant is **Miller Freeman**, a company founded in 1902 that originally specialized in natural resource industries but has broadened into a wide variety of industry markets, including the lucrative computer, electronics, construction, information technology and health care industries.

Miller Freeman, based in San Francisco, also publishes over 100 magazines and 40 directories in Europe from its London subsidiary, Miller Freeman plc. Miller Freeman Asia publishes about 40 magazines and directories in Hong Kong, Singapore and Kuala Lampur. Although I have never had a single problem with the company in terms of copyrights, such a global spread is becoming common in the trade magazine industry, and especially with the proliferation of online versions of trade magazines. Writers must take special care to understand what rights they are selling and be ready to stick to their agreement and have the publisher do the same.

Penton Publishing is also a highly respected publisher of trade magazines. Some of its flagship publications reach more than 150,000 readers—a higher circulation than many national consumer publications. It has publications covering construction, hospitality, manufacturing, metals, and distribution. *Industry Week*, its flagship publication, is a must for managers in major manufacturing companies, and sister publication, *IW Growing Companies*, is followed closely by managers in smaller manufacturing firms. In one sense, these two publications are "business press," but they are actually targeting what could be called the "management" industry.

Penton has nine divisions whose flagship magazines include: A/E/C *Systems, Design Mart* and *Electronic Design* in the design field; *Restaurant Hospitality* and *LH* (*Lodging Hospitality*) in the hospitality industry; *Government Product News* in the government procurement market; *Internet World* in the electronic information market; *American Machinist* and *NC Shop Owner* in the metals industry; *Contracting Business* and *HPAC* (*Heating/Piping/Air Conditioning*) in construction; and *Transportation & Distribution* and *Material Handling Engineering* in the distribution industry.

Another giant, **Ziff-Davis Inc.**, defines verticality. From its basic winner, *PC Computing*, which is something between a trade magazine and a specialty publication, the company has developed a range of trade and specialty magazines that reach into every nook and cranny of computer applications and information technology

Given this base to build on, Ziff-Davis has forged ahead to new frontiers with free online newsletters, twenty-one as we write, and a variety of other electronic and print products which offer many opportunities to trade writers who have a bent for computing.

We've spent some time with the high profile publishers, but there are many other large firms with multiple books that need to be mentioned.

Ziff-Davis's main competition comes from **IDG** (International Data Group) which publishes the popular *PC World*. With more than 290 publications in75 countries, IDG claims to be the world's leading publisher of computer magazines and newspapers, a claim that few would dispute. Some of its largest titles include *Macworld, InfoWorld, Network World, Channel World*, but also such highly targeted trades as *Computer Reseller, Federal Computer Week, Publish, CIO*, and *Info-Tech Magazine* in Canada.

The good news for trade writers is that articles can be easily translated for publication in other IDG publications. That's also the bad news, because you must be careful about what rights you are agreeing to sell. And with the overburdening presence of on-line editions, especially with a computer-savvy publisher such as IDG, your best protection is to read the contract BEFORE you sign it.

IDG also has a claim to fame as a book publisher of interest to some trade writers because it produces the popular "...for Dummies" series.

Advanstar covers application technology, art, beauty, call centers, energy, entertainment and marketing, fashion, healthcare, information technology, landscaping, motor vehicle, OEM processing, paper, pest control, pharmaceuticals, science and technology, telecommunications, travel and hospitality.

Bill Communications, a subsidiary of VNU USA, the North American arm of the Netherlands-based communications company, focuses on sales and marketing management,

73

event planning, plastics, automotive, assisted living, hospitality, apparel, information management, retailing, and food processing, retailing and service.

BPI Communications, also a VNU subsidiary, is a kingpin in the coverage of the entertainment and media industries with books such as *Billboard, AdWeek* and *American Artist*, but it also hits the design and construction markets with Interiors and Architecture, and support markets for entertainment, media, and yes construction, with publications such as PDN (Photo District News).

Business Communications Company, Inc., primarily publishes newsletters and technical journals rather than trade magazines, but they do accept the occasional freelance piece. More to the point, if you are following a cutting edge high-tech industry other than computers, you probably will want to look at some of the information they provide in areas such as genetic research, battery and fuel cell development, medical materials and much more. If you are interested in science-oriented trade writing, BCC also offers opportunities with special reports which they retail for between $1500 and $4000. Depending on the contract you negotiate, this could be a lucrative side for trade and technical writers.

Business News Publishing is my kind of company because they have a tremendous list of publications for construction and construction materials with such industry leaders as *Walls & Ceilings* (interiors), *Stone World, SNIPS* (sheet metal contractors), *PHC Profit Report, Plumbing and Mechanical, Floor Covering Installer, Roofing Contractor*—twenty-seven publications by my count.

Canon Communications focuses on the medical products and device industry with publications such as *Medical Device & Diagnostic Industry, Medical Product Manufacturing News, IVD Technology, Medical Electronics Manufacturing and*

Medical Plastics and Biomaterials.

CMP Media is a competitor for Ziff-Davis and a good one. Their flagship publication is *BYTE*, but *Information Week , Network Computing, Computer Retail Week, Datacommunications, PlanetIT, UNIX World,* and *Electronic Buyers News* all enjoy a very good reputation within their industries. Along with *BYTE, Windows Magazine* has become a staple for the consumer market as well.

Well know as publishers of automotive repair books, **Chilton** is also a major trade magazine publisher with a wide range of magazine targeted, naturally, to the automotive and transportation industries, but also with leading publications applying to manufacturing operations in a range of industries such as *Manufacturing Systems, Food Engineering, Industrial Maintenance and Plant Operation, Industrial Safety & Hygiene, Jewelers' Circular-Keystone,* and in healthcare with *Review of Ophthalmology* and *Review of Optometry.*

Commerce Publishing Company specializes in the retail and insurance industries with magazines such as *American Agent & Broker* and *Life Insurance Selling,* and *Decor* and *Art Buyers Caravan.*

Elsevier Science, part of publishing giant Reed-Elsevier, primarily publishes journals of science and medicine. Most of these are peer-reviewed journals that offer little opportunity for freelance writers except in the area of editing articles for contributors.

Fairchild Publications, owned by the American Broadcasting Company, focuses on the apparel industry with leading titles such as *Women's Wear Daily* and *Daily News Record* (for menswear), and the retail grocers' industry with *Supermarket News.*

Gulf Publishing is a leader in trade magazines for the oil and gas industry. Some of its leading titles are *Oil & Gas Technology, Pipe Line & Gas Industry, Hydrocarbon Processing,* and *World Oil.*

Hart Publications is a division of Phillips Business Information, Inc. Like Gulf Publications, Hart's strength is in the oil and gas industry with such successful titles as *Oil and Gas Investor, Oil and Gas World, Petroleum Engineer International,* and *Lubricants World.*

The forest products industry is covered by **Hatton-Brown Publishers, Inc.**, which produces *Timber Harvesting, Timber Products, Southern Loggin' Times* and *Panel World.* Additionally the company produces *Power Equipment Trade* for independent lawn and garden dealers in the U.S. For Harley-Davidson enthusiasts, it also produces one consumer specialty magazine, *Iron Works.*

Speaking of consumer specialty magazines, trade writers should also be aware of the specialty magazines published by the **Hearst Corporation** which include such well known titles as *Popular Mechanics, Harper's Bazaar, Good Housekeeping, Country Living, Motor Boating & Sailing* and more including widely popular consumer publications, *Cosmopolitan* and *Esquire.* The specialty magazines, particularly the ever changing myriad of shelter publications and special issues revolving around *Good Housekeeping* and *Country Living,* offer the trade writer a chance to expand their markets and visibility, a subject we'll cover later.

ISC, Inc., is a leading publisher of scientific journals and tabloids covering biotechnology, clinical disciplines, and environmental testing laboratories. In North America it produces publications such as *American Laboratory, American Biotechnology Laboratory, American Clinical Laboratory, American Environmental Laboratory,* and *Managing the Modern Laboratory.* It also publishes in Europe and Asian markets.

Lebhar-Friedman is a leading publisher in the retail trade with titles such as *Chain Store Age, Drug Store News, Home Center News, Restaurant News,* and *Discount Store News.*

Lippincott Williams & Wilkins publishes trade periodicals targeting the medical industry and its professions. Most of its publications are peer-reviewed journals, but is important for medical writers to be aware of because it is a prolific publisher of monographs and books as well. In fact, LWW may be the fastest growing of all the trade publishing companies as this book goes to press.

Perhaps of more interest to article writers is the **Medical Economics Company** which not only publishes trade magazines and books but also consumer guides of various kinds—the ones you find in a doctor's office. For trade writers who don't specialize in the science of medicine, Medical Economics Company covers a wide range of health care business in titles such as *Assisted Living Business Report, BioWorld Financial Watch, Business & Health, Case Management Advisor, Cost Management in Cardiac Care, Dental Practice & Finance, Employee Health & Fitness, Healthcare Purchasing News, Healthcare Risk Management* and many, many more.

Meriod Corporation also produces seventeen Advance magazines that serve different medical disciplines with titles such as *Health Information Executives, Occupational Therapy Practitioners, Medical Laboratory Professionals, Nurse Practitioners, Physicians Assistants* and more. Most articles are written by practitioners, but some come from medical writing specialists who aren't practicing professionals.

Miller Publishing Company's publications revolve around the forestry industry, but go beyond into the products produced from trees, including the *Import/Export Wood Purchasing News,* the *National Hardwood Magazine,* and *The Softwood Forest Products Buyer.*

Mosby is a trade journal producer for the medical, nursing, dental and allied health industries, but some of their journals sit on the border between journal and trade magazine. *Home Care Provider* and *Nursing Outlook* offer the most opportunity to place articles that aren't peer-reviewed.

National Business Magazines, Inc., produces magazines that cover the commercial graphics industry with everything from *AutoGraphics* and *Restyling* for automotive graphics to *Promowear* and *Printwear* in the silkscreen industry to *Digital Graphics* for large format digital printers to *Screen Graphics* and *Sign Business* as well as *A&E*, a magazine for the awards and engraving industry.

North American Publishing covers the printing side of the publishing industry with magazines that cover packaging, marketing, graphics, direct mail, magazine and bookselling, mailing, and form printing as well as media directories. It also produces products for the consumer electronics industry.

Odyssey Group produces publications that, for lack of a better way to put it, cover the enthusiast industry. It's premier magazines are *Autograph Collector Magazine* and *Pop Culture Collecting Magazine*.

PennWell Publications produces more than 39 trade magazines and newsletter in industries from energy and electric power to healthcare to information technology. This is one of the major publishers to know about if you are serious about building a freelance trade writing career. Some of their titles include *Clean Rooms, Military & Aerospace Electronics, Solid State Technology, Industrial Laser Solutions, Vision Systems Design, Electronic Publishing, Energy Marketing, Utility Automation, Dental Economics, Offshore Magazine, Oil & Gas Journal, Fire Engineering,* and *Water World.*

Petersen Publishing Company, although not a trade magazine publisher, publishing specialty magazines of interest to trade writers in the automotive, electronics, and sports retailing industry with title such as *Home Theater Interiors, Portable Computing, Mobile Computing, Motor Trend, Truck Trend, Kit Car, Inline Retailer, Bike, Dive Report,* and *Surfer.*

Phillips Publishing covers aviation, finance, and technology with titles such as *Aviation Today, Technology Investing, Wireless Today, Cable Today,* the *ISP Business News,* and the Hart Energy Publications previously mentioned.

Preston Publications focuses on the marine industry with *Boat Motor Dealer, Marina Dock Age,* and *Recreational Boating News* which straddles the line between trade and consumer. *Photo Techniques Magazines* is primarily for professional photographers. It also publishes two scientific peer-review journals, *Analytical Toxicology* and *Chromatographic Science.*

Quest Publishing Company publishes *Treatment Today* for the behavioral health and addiction treatment fields.

Randall Publishing controls the Construction Media Group and its *Equipment World* is one of the premier magazines for the heavy equipment industry. It also has top titles for the trucking/shipping industry with *Trucking Co.* for small trucking companies, *Overdrive* which serves owner-operators and fleet managers, and *Truckers News* for drivers. *RentSmart!* covers the construction rental industry.

Although **Rodale Press** is primarily a consumer publications publisher, trade writers will find opportunities for crossover articles on health, outdoor recreation, residential construction and agriculture.

RP Publishing serves the alternative fuels industry and the companion animal field. Standard titles include *Propane Vehicle Magazine* and *Natural Gas Fuels Magazine,* and *World*

Natural Gas Fuels Magazine. RP Publishing also publishes a consumer magazine for parents.

Scranton Gillette Communications is well know for its titles covering the heavy/highway construction industry. **Roads & Bridges** is its flagship magazine, but *Water Engineering & Management, Water & Wastes Digest, Seed World,* and *Greenhouse Product News* are also well recognized in their fields. It also publishes *The Diapason,* the official journal of the International Society for Organ History and Preservation. These are organs that you play, not organs that keep you alive. Now that's specializing.

SLACK Incorporated publishes healthcare information, education and association management products and services. Its journal publishing division produces more than 30 "independent and society-owned" publications in the medical field. Among these are newspaper formats such as *Cardiology Today, Infectious Disease News, Ocular Surgery News* and more. Although journals are peer-reviewed, a couple of titles accept advertising and walk the border between magazine and journal.

Sosland Publishing is a leading trade publisher for the food and food processing industry, particularly with grain-based foods. Among its top titles are *Milling & Baking News, Baking & Snack, World Grain, Meat & Poultry,* and *Bakery Production & Marketing Newsletter.*

With *Fine Woodworking* and *Fine Homebuilding,* **The Taunton Press** has proven a trade magazine can move into the consumer field anytime an interest develops beyond the industry practitioner. After all, the majority of the folks actually using the techniques in those two magazines are trade craftsmen and business owners, but hey, it doesn't hurt to drool over that beautifully crafted wood and those tools I'll never master does it? Again, Taunton certainly offers an opportunity for crossover articles.

Testa Communications concentrates on the communications industry's various aspects with titles ranging from *DJ Times* for radio jocks to *Sound & Communications* for A/V contractors. Some top titles include *Music and Sound Retailer, Producer,* and *Stage & Studio.*

Like many modern trade magazine publishers, **Vance Publishing** began in 1937 with one magazine. Now it is divided into six operating division, each with several publications. A leader in agricultural magazines, Vance has three agricultural divisions: Livestock, Crops, and Produce. The livestock division includes *Drovers Journal* which is 125 years old. It's industrial division has leading publications on furniture, cabinetry and wood products, which ties in well with the Decor Division covering residential interior retail. The Salon Division divisions covers every element for a retail salon owner, and the Supermarket Retail Division's magazines extend the business cycle begun in agriculture.

Privately held, **Virgo Publishing, Inc.**, specializes in "niche-market opportunities" with magazines on telecommunications, the embroidery trade, self-storage, sports licensing, outdoor products, advertising specialties, libraries, event management, haberdasheries and more.

Although not a trade magazine publisher, **Warren, Gorham & Lamont** is an important publisher for writers who focus on the finance industry. They are a leading firm in publishing journals, manuals, and books on corporate finance issues and taxation.

Watt Publishing Company publishes agricultural industry publications in poultry, meat processing, feed and pet food. With top titles such as *Poultry Digest, Turkey World, Pet Food Industry, Meat Processing,* and *Feed Management,* Watt publishes worldwide with specific editions for specific regions.

Webb Farm Press is actually a division of Intertec, but its publications are such an important resource to the agricultural industry that they are worth separate mention. The subsidiary produces both national and regional publications with titles such as *Beef, Farm Industry News, Soybean Digest,* and *National Hog Farmer,* but adapt articles to regional books such as *California-Arizona Farm Press, Delta Farm Press, Southwest Farm Press,* and *Southeast Farm Press,* all of which are regional weeklies in tabloid format.

There you have a brief—and let me stress the "brief"—round up of most prominent of trade magazine publishers. If you didn't see a title covering your field, don't despair. For one thing, this chapter didn't provide enough room to go into detail for all of these firms; and for another, as you look at every large publisher listed here, often several local and regional publishers for these industries exist.

Finding specialized trade magazines in your area can often be as easy as looking in the phone directory under "Periodicals, Publishers." By networking within an industry, you'll find your acquaintances and sources are reading publications you have never heard of, but should contact. In my region, for example, a wonderful bi-monthly publication entitled *UTAD News* covers the advertising and public relations industry in Salt Lake City. The issues cover not only agencies, but also vendors and venues, so it is prized by the media and their vendors here. And yes, it does provide an opportunity for freelance writers.

So check your neighborhood first. The best advice is to learn about an industry in your own locale first because it will provide you with the resources you need. If you don't find an industry publication locally, the next sources to check are Bacon's Directory, the Gebbie Directory, and Standard Rate and Data Service's *Business Rates and Data,* vol. II, and *Healthcare Publications,* vol 3. Consumer publications take up volume I, so that should tell you a bit about what you've been missing for market opportunities.

Chapter 5

How to get the maximum information in the least amount of time from the people you interview.

Develop a research plan.

When I was a kid, I hated to write essays in school. Typically, when you got to class, the teacher would tell everyone to write a 250 to 500 word essay on the spot about the pros and cons, say, on driving cars or pollution or smoking or some such notion. Remember how hard it was to hit that magic number of words even if you were the most glib kid in class? The reason: You hadn't done any research, so what you were coming up with was whatever thoughts and facts you had in your head about that subject at the time. If you had never thought about smoking, pollution or driving, the writing was difficult.

The purpose of research may be to get the facts straight, but for a practical writer, research is also the means of figuring out what to write about. As a general rule of thumb, the more research you can do, the easier the writing goes.

The real question for productive writers, however, is how

much research is enough, and how much is too much or too little.

If you've gone through a particular magazine to see what the editor wants, you already have a starting point for planning your research. You've noted how many sources, both human and non, were quoted, where they were from, and how they were used to back up a point.

Now it's time to work on a research outline you can live with for the story. What I mean by "live with" is simple: How much time can you spend researching an article and still make the hourly rate you deserve? Let's say that you want to make $30 per hour from your writing. At $30 per hour, you will actually clear something closer to $14, but that's still a decent enough take home to make writing more worthwhile than working at a convenience store. If the article you are shooting for is going to pay $300, then simple division tells you that if you put about 10 hours into the research, writing, rewriting, and photography on the article, you'll make the rate you want. If you must put in more than 10 hours, you'll come out with a lower rate, and if you put in less than 10 hours, your rate of pay will effectively go up.

Knowing how many hours you can spend on a piece is really the first step in planning your research. The plan must balance the needs of the article—the amount of information your analysis of the magazine tells you the editor must have—against your personal need to make a fair amount for your time.

For most trade stories, the most cost-effective research is interviews.

I can't emphasize that point enough. Many of us are shy and bit retiring, so the notion of interviewing can be a bit frightening, especially when we must talk to someone that we don't know. The trouble is, even with the Internet, finding printed facts is time-consuming at best, and time spent looking for written materials can quickly drop that $30 per hour rate down to $10 or $8 or $5 per hour.

Let's say your analysis of a basic feature for the target magazine shows the editor prefers an average of four interviews, and that at least two paragraphs of a typical feature appears to have background information found in written sources (don't count the apropos Emerson quote you're planning to use).

Okay, four interviews. How long will that take? Depends. If you are going to call each of them, figure about a half-hour of wasted time with each as you play phone tag, then figure about an hour with each doing the interview, so for four interviews, your total time is probably four hours plus two hours phone tag for a total of six hours.

Now this smaller magazine is only paying you $300 per story, so after six hours of work, you have just four hours left to write the article and edit it. But what if you have to meet each interviewee at their office? How long does the drive time take to and from? Even if they are close, it probably adds another couple of hours, and then you are down to two hours to write and edit the story. All of a sudden, you start to decide that you'll probably bring in about $20 per hour on this story (to give yourself an extra five hours).

What's a professional to do?

First, plan your questions so that the hour interview only takes about thirty minutes. You do need to spend a little "rapport" time with each interviewee to make them feel both comfortable with your professionalism and comfortable with being interviewed, but truthfully, if you have a carefully planned sequence of questions, you can do the typical phone interview in about thirty to forty-five minutes. If you find yourself going longer, you're probably having too much conversation and not enough questioning.

Second, aim for a phone interview if possible, and if you must go to the interviewee's office for the interview, try to combine that visit with as many business-related chores as possible, such as other interviews nearby or trips for supplies or a trip to the library.

Third, start thinking about additional articles to additional non-competitive markets. If you can do an hour interview once and put quotations and information from it into four different articles, then you are effectively putting only a quarter hour's worth into the $300 initial article, not an hour.

A variety of good books exist on the techniques of interviewing, Michael Schumacher's *The Writer's Complete Guide to Conducting Interviews*, and an excellent chapter in Hank Nuwer's *How To Write Like An Expert About Anything*. The drawback to their advice is that their books assume you have unlimited time to prepare for and conduct the interview. I will tell you from experience: you don't. You have, as a practical matter if you want to make a few dollars from your writing, about twenty to thirty minutes to prepare questions and about thirty to forty minutes to conduct the interview.

Prepare some, but not all, of your questions beforehand. The problem with information is that it is seldom found altogether. That is to say, there's a bit over here, and a bit over there, and even more in this spot, and less in another spot. The majority of your job in an interview is to take the interviewee to all the spots you need to go, but not to every spot in the entire universe.

This can be a true challenge. Some interviewees only want to go to certain spots. It's not necessarily that they have anything to hide. More often, they just want to be "on the safe side." The safe side can be anything from a natural modesty or even shyness about their company's accomplishments to outright lying about whether their company just dumped a thousand barrels of oil onto a coastline.

When you prepare questions ahead of time, the mere process gets you thinking about what you want out of the interview. At a minimum, you need questions of who, what, where, why and how. But additionally, you need to discover where your interviewee is on the information ladder. Going back to Clinton's notion of an information pyramid, remember that users stand underneath makers, and makers often stand underneath developers, so if you are doing a story on, say, an uninterrupted power supply for a computer room, your interview may lead your source to suggest you talk to the manufacturer of the equipment who may push you upward to the designer.

Even with carefully prepared questions, frequently the interview will take you in other directions from where you intended to go. By all means, be willing to go there provided you don't lose sight of the who, what, where, when, why, and how you needed in the first place.

To me, the ability to allow an interview flexibility is the secret to making multiple sales. If you understand the advantage of writing as many stories as possible from the same body of research, you'll appreciate that your interviewee may be helping you develop new topics. A case in point. Recently I was interviewing an electrical engineer about a specific audio/visual system he had designed for a local company. As he was describing the system, he had a habit of saying that a similar system was used on the so and so project.

As the interview finished, I had not only all the basic questions answered for the current article I was working on, but also the basic questions answered to query for three other stories, two of which were assigned immediately.

How to prepare for an interview

There are a couple of ways you can go about preparing questions for an interview. The most pragmatic, I think, is to prepare a "grid" of questions. Down the side of the grid, list the "who, what, where, when, why, and how" and across the top of the grid, list the types of people you need to interview.

It's the people across the top of the grid that help tell you what basic questions to ask. Another example from construction. If I'm asked to do a general project story, my list of interviewees starts with the general contractor (actually his project manager, the guy who oversees the contracts so that everyone is paid). Knowing how the construction process works, the next two on the list are, in order, the architect and the owner.

Because I understand the industry, I start with the general contractor because I know he will have the names of everyone up and down the project. If all I have is the owner, the owner may only know the architect and general contractor directly, although generally the large owners and their representatives will know everyone as well.

Based on the interview with the general contractor as to who, etc., I may add others to the list to interview, most often the structural engineer or steel erector, the mechanical contractor or the electrical contractor. Often that leads to yet another sub-subcontractor such as the plumbing contractor or the controls installer.

If it is a different type of story, though, the grid can change radically. On an issue piece about the changing nature of construction contracts, the grid would be radically different along the top, beginning with a good construction lawyer, then a trade association executive, and then moving into interviews with general contractors and subcontractors. If the story is about equipment rental, it might start with the general contractor, but would not include either the owner or architect since they have little to do with equipment rental except in extremely unusual circumstances.

When you are looking for the right sources, the ones who are keys to the information you need, go back to your analysis of the magazine you are writing for. Chances are that sources you find in past stories are still willing and able to answer new questions that will help your story along. At least notice the types of professions being interviewed.

What do you need to know? Any non-fiction article, trade or otherwise, can be broken down easily into certain categories of information. The list includes anecdotes, background information, "context", explanations, facts, narration, reactions or evaluations, and statements of position or belief.

For articles of five hundred words or less, you are going to be concentrating on facts. At most you can deal with one item from the above list in five hundred words (i.e. a single anecdote developed or a single evaluation or a single statement of a position). On articles above five hundred words, you have some room for narration, evaluation, background, context and statements although common sense tells you the less space you have, the more likely you will narrow these choices. You may, for instance, start off with an anecdote that may provide both background and context, and then complete the article with facts and a brief evaluation.

On the whole, though, for the vast majority of short articles, you want specific facts with a few informative reactions from interviewees. Again, who-what-when stands you in good stead.

Longer articles beg for more flesh as well as more bone. To get both, you must use a technique called probing. Probing means asking your interviewee to amplify their answer, sometimes redirecting the interviewee to pick up a thread from earlier in the interview or sometimes widening the overall focus. Often interviewees will amplify on their own as you develop the fine art of being interested but saying nothing. Nature abhors a vacuum; conversationalists abhor a silence. When the interviewee is on a roll, you can maintain the stimulation by murmering encouragement such as "I see" or "What happened next?"

A second element of probing is asking for clarification. In trade writing, you are frequently facing the unknown. You're an outsider, not an engineer or a doctor or a computer programmer. As the interviewee blasts you with the idiom of the industry, you may not have a clue what's being said, or maybe you just want to verify that you do. Asking your source to define a word, especially an acronym, or asking what they mean is perfectly acceptable,and usually leads to elaboration that is useful.

One thing to avoid, though, is criticism. Never tell an interviewee that he or she isn't being clear. Criticism implies a lack of objectivity on your part. Always point out that it is *you* that doesn't understand. Most folks understand it is in their best interest to have you understand exactly what they are saying. When it isn't in their best interest, you can use a third approach to probing: confrontation.

I don't mean the same kind of confrontation you see on

the network news shows where Mike Wallace or Sam Donaldson is trying to trip up someone in a false statement. (That, too, may have its place depending on the story). Confrontation in most interviews is simply pointing out inconsistencies between what the interviewee has told you and the facts, or what the interviewee had previously said and what is being said now.

You can take the combative edge from this type of probe by putting the onus again on your own understanding of the facts or of what was previously said. Sometimes you are going to ask "hard" questions, questions that will be seen as critical or even threatening. Sometimes you must ask these questions as a matter of fairness, allowing the interviewee to respond to an allegation by someone else. Sometimes, the facts all point to mistakes that you have to inquire about. My advice, when you must ask such questions, is to try to build some rapport with the interviewee first and save the hard questions until late in the interview because frequently such questions will mean the end of the interviewee's cooperation.

Patterns for useful questions

Open-ended questions. "The difference between a thoughtful, properly worded question and a sloppy, poorly worded question is the difference between a clear, complete answer and a vague or incomplete answer," says Michael Schumacher in *The Writer's Complete Guide to Conducting Interviews.* Open-ended questions are designed to generate lengthier, thoughtful answers.

Such questions also help the interviewee understand what needs to be explained and encourages them to "loosen up." Most interviews depend on open-ended questions for effectiveness which is why such questions generally start with the 'how" and the "why" in your basic question grid.

If all you did was ask open-ended questions, however, you'd probably never finish an interview, or you'd finish it much more quickly than you want to. Since open-ended questions tend to encourage a lengthier response, too many can actually lead some interviewees right off the topic. For those interviewees who are somewhat shy, open-ended questions can be a bit intimidating: They are being asked to talk more than their psychological make-up will tolerate.

A good interview mixes in closed questions that require brief, simple responses. A closed question either requires a simple yes or no, or offers the interviewee two choices of response. Large or small? Long or short? Pre-cast or poured-in-place? UBC or BOCA?

Make sure the choice is appropriate, though, because a closed question can have implications even in the simple "yes" or "no." I once heard a interviewer ask a contractor if he had stopped bid shopping—a common but reprehensible practice where the contractor "shops" the award of the project to any sub who will give him the lowest price, even after using some other sub's bid to win the project. The red-faced contractor had no good way to answer. A "yes" implied he had been bid shopping. A "no" implied he was currently bid shopping. The actual response was to take a swing at the interviewer.

Problematic questions. Developing a rapport with the interviewee is an essential part of getting honest, helpful information. Some types of questions, like the one mentioned above, have built-in problems. The main problem, though, is that they destroy your credibility with the interviewee and in the process, the interviewee's willingness to help you understand, to lead you to further information sources, and to expand and clarify. Some of these problematic questions include:

• Leading questions. "Didn't you already know the meaning of 'is' when you said it depends on what the meaning of 'is' is?" Leading questions are those that imply you already have an opinion and just want to verify your point of view. That's not to say it isn't okay to verify information. It is. But leading questions, so popular in movies with trials, as well as presidential grand jury depositions, will quickly make your interviewee suspect your intentions and motives for the interview. As a matter of practical psychology, people will be more open when they believe they are *teaching* you something new than when they are asked to verify the answer you already think you have.

• Obvious or just plain stupid questions. The old adage is that there is no such thing as a stupid question, but all of us know better. If you think you are going to ask an obvious question, at least let the interviewee know that, while the answer may be obvious to him, your lack of understanding about the situation makes it an answer you need.

Of course, there's the rub. The question may not seem that obvious to you. "Why is there a steel contractor if the bridge is held up by concrete beams and columns?" Well, almost anyone in the construction industry—from an interior designer to a painter's assistant—knows that load-bearing concrete has to be reinforced with steel rebar, hence the steel contractor. Often a little study into the subject will remove such annoying questions from your list of things to ask. That's one of the prime reasons you need to find a mentor for every field you want to cover.

• Multiple choice questions. The problem with multiple choice questions is that so often they are a disguised form of verifying a preconceived idea. If you ask a project manager in construction whether the project is design/build or hard bid, you will probably get one or the other as an answer when actually the project is more likely these days to be a hybrid.

Multiple choice questions, especially those beginning with "either/or" or "whether or not" actually tend to be more vague than you might suspect because they give the interviewee a ready answer, one that needs no explanation, and therefore, no clarification.

As a general rule, avoid multiple choice questions unless the interviewee has set up the defining terms for you. For example, you might discover in the course of an interview that a retailer has three defining keys he uses to determine when to set up a display. As he shows you around some recent displays, you can certainly ask which of the three keys was most important in deciding on this type of display or that. The main thing to remember is to avoid using a multiple choice question as a leading question.

• Don't apologize. Interviewers who are new to a field often find themselves saying, "I hate to ask, but . . ." or "Pardon me, but . . ." as a way of either softening the hard question they are about to ask or apologizing for what seems, even to them, a stupid question.

From the interviewee's side, however, opening a question with an apology is like a red flag—it generates either fear (how is the answer going to be used?) or loathing (if you hate to ask, don't) whether you are in Las Vegas or not. A better tactic, if the question is on the foolish side, is to soften after the question by saying, "Boy that was a dumb question, wasn't it." If you are asking a hard question, however, you are most likely trying to probe for more elaborate or definitive responses, so don't try to soften the question, but if the interviewee is reluctant to answer, you might try explaining why the answer is going to be important to the image the interviewee projects in the article.

Managing interviews for productivity

Sometimes the right source is unavailable, either in person or by phone. This situation can be difficult to handle. Basically, your next step is to contact an assistant to see if the person you need to interview can contact you rather than you spending time chasing them down. This is seldom ideal, and I've played the game of phone tag several times trying to arrange such a call. It's especially difficult if the interviewee is out of the country, not just out of town.

Two options are either to fax or to e-mail your questions with enough information about when you need a response so that you can give the interviewee a sense of urgency. However, this method is seldom adequate because you are building no rapport with the interviewee. My advice is to find a substitute for the interviewee if at all possible. If the story must center on the interviewee, the other tactic is to interview as many information sources around the interviewee's subject as possible so that you can meld the limited answers into a story you've built through information provided by other sources.

Is this cheating the reader? Probably. Is it a fact of the writing life? Absolutely. As a general rule, though, I've found company officers are much more understanding about deadlines and the need to reply to a faxed set of questions than are subordinates further down in the command chain. Top executives are also much more likely to elaborate on their answers without much prodding—most of them have a sense that trade articles, as opposed to newspaper articles—are unlikely to have an agenda to ruin them or their company, and in fact are often a way to boost their image for recruiting personnel and new customers.

An alternative is to ask your editor if you can delay the story to accommodate the interview. I think trade editors are much more approachable with this idea than are consumer editors who have dialed in their calendar. For one thing, consumer editors generally can draw from a wider range of backup from writers waiting in the wings. Trade magazines seldom have such a backup potential, but because they don't, they often plan their editorial calendar with more flexibility.

All you can do is ask, and if the answer is no, then your best bet is to explain the difficulties and suggest shifting the slant a bit to adapt to the circumstances.

Post-interview etiquette. If you've taken up a substantial amount of time with an interviewee, it's always politic to send a note or letter thanking interviewees for being so cooperative and giving of their time. Remember that any industry is a small world. You will work with that interviewee again, most likely, and even if you don't, I promise you the time will come when their good opinion of the way you work will earn you either a different interview or an assignment.

On shorter interviews, you may not want to go to all the trouble of a formal note, but you can always fax a handwritten thank you. Since I often fax a draft of the article to the people I interview so they can help check the accuracy of facts in the story and of their quotation, I generally include my thanks for their time and cooperation on the fax cover sheet.

Should you always fax back a draft of the article. No. But the best journalists always check their facts and also their quotations. If this means just calling the interviewee and reading back just their quotations, it also gives you an opportunity to thank them again.

And if the interviewee wants to change something in your article or in the quote you've read back to them, remember it is your call. As a rule of thumb, I will allow interviewees to modify their quote or elaborate on it as long as the gist is the same, and I will certainly allow them to correct mistaken factual information such as square footage or the number of cranes used or whatnot.

The areas that are off-limits, and I make this clear, are the story's organization, its slant, its grammar and syntax, and its stylistic conventions. I've seldom found anyone short of an editor who understands the working differences between AP style, the Chicago Manual of Style, and the magazine's in-house style guide, even if I have interviewed several people who are probably better writers than me. No one, however, will ever know the requirements of your story better than you do.

I also transcribe quite a few interviews, especially for longer stories. Very often I will fax the entire transcription to a company's marketing office (especially if they have helped me get the interview). Why do that? Very often the public relations and marketing people find they can use quotations from such a transcription in their materials as well, and to be honest, it is an inexpensive way of maintaining a good relationship for future stories.

Tape or notes? Truly, this isn't an either/or question. Without question you should tape every interview if possible for a couple of reasons. First, the advantage of being able to replay exactly what was said is valuable. Second, it allows you an opportunity to evaluate your own interviewing technique so that you can improve.

That said, taping an interview is still no substitution for notes. The problem I have with notes is that I write very slowly in longhand. At best my notes must stay cryptic because there isn't a chance that I'll be able to write fast enough to keep up with someone speaking. But tapes break, batteries die, people mumble—all are reasons you must supplement what you tape with notes. Another advantage is that notes give you a shorthand table of contents to help you find specific areas on the taped interview.

Should you make a full transcription of the interview? The answer is both yes and no. Remember, you are trying to work cost-effectively, so transcribing the interview yourself adds to the time you put into the article. Having someone else transcribe the interview adds an expense that comes out of your pocket and lessens the amount of "take home" you get from the article.

On the other hand, transcribing refreshes your memory and lets you nail the quotation exactly because you have written it down exactly as it was said. My personal practice is to transcribe the majority of the interviews I do if I hope to use the information in more than one article or if the interview is short enough that it won't take much time. Fortunately I can type almost as fast as most interviewees speak, so that's a definite advantage. If you are the hunt and peck sort, though, you have some obstacles to overcome.

If I don't think material from the interview will be used elsewhere, I may play the tape of the interview as I am writing the story and just cue up any good quotations so I can transcribe them directly into the story. Also, I listen to portions of the interview to make sure my notes are accurate and to pick out any specific wording that I didn't get down in full while I was taking notes. My strength is typing, my weakness is taking notes. Those facts determine my procedure, and your strengths should determine yours.

Should I "fix" a quotation from someone whose grammar is less than pristine? You can safely fix syntax in most cases, but you be careful not to put words in someone else's mouth. This can be a bit difficult. During the heat of an interview, you're getting all kinds of non-verbal communications that carry context. When you sit down to transcribe, though, you find the subject used the word "stuff" at various times to mean "procedures," "equipment," "administrative difficulties," "OSHA regulations," and a variety of other things. During the interview, you had no trouble understanding what "stuff" meant, but Murphy's Law says that if you put in the words you understood "stuff" to mean, you're subject will complain.

That's one reason why you should always run at least your quotation past the person you interviewed even if you don't show them the entire story. In the "good old days" of magazines and newspapers, according to legend, there were fact checkers who checked every fact. I suspect this is as much myth as truth except in the largest organizations. At any rate, with the lean, mean staffing on modern magazines, it has become your responsibility to check facts and to make sure you are quoting accurately.

Showing or not showing a copy of the article to those who have been interviewed is something of an ethical dilemma. On the one hand, you need to be accurate. On the other, you can't accept censorship. Each article, I've discovered, has its own set of factors that must be considered:

1. **Is it investigative?** My rule of thumb on investigative pieces—which I honestly avoid like the plague because they are both difficult to pull of with assurance and because they are so time-consuming. You seldom get an adequate monetary pay-off although you may get a spiritual one. My rule is to pass only the quotation past the interviewee and give them an opportunity to be sure they were clearly and fairly quoted.

2. **Are competitors involved?** A more likely scenario in trade magazine journalism is that you are doing a piece where competitors are involved. If showing the draft of the article could possibly give any competitor a business advantage before the piece is published, then your fairest course is to check facts verbally and to check quotations. Once the article runs, of course, the combatants are on their own. It's not your job to keep someone from giving away the farm to a competitor, but

it is your job to keep the pigs in the pen until the sale is made.

3. **Have you set up the topic fairly for the interviewee?** To be productive, you must always try to sell your research more than once, but in doing so, sometimes the change of slant in the subject between one market and another also changes the shade of meaning in a quotation. While there's no hard and fast rule regarding this situation, my personal preference is to contact the interviewee and ask a fresh question on exactly the subject you are writing about.

Remember that it is a small world according to Murphy's Law. In investigative journalism, it is fair game not to let someone know they are about to get the shaft. In information journalism, you will probably be going to the same contacts again and again and again. The reputation you want to build is for being fair without being a pushover. When sources believe you treat them fairly, they generally will continue to be good sources for information, even if something they were quoted as saying has given them difficulties in their business or professional life. Most understand the choice was theirs to say or not say what they were thinking. If they believe you treated them fairly, more often than not they will continue to be good sources of information, albeit more circumspect.

Chapter 6

How to learn the trade writing craft with case histories, project profiles, and other "on the scene" stories.

The staple of most trade magazines is what I like to think of as the "on the scene" story. These include case histories, site visits, project reports, and profiles of what an individual company is doing.

By extending the concept, you could include stories about trade shows or association meetings—you certainly have to be on the scene to report on these events—but generally these stories have a different structure and tone. Frequently such stories are essentially straight reporting—you try to present the facts of the event that took place, but you make little or no attempt to evaluate the event. By contrast, "on the scene" stories focus on evaluating the facts of a project or process or company, which is why they are a valuable part of the magazine for the reader.

For the writer, it's important to remember that the goal of any trade magazine is to help the reader *do* something. When you visit a scene—a construction site, an operating theater, a food packaging line, a printing plant, a commercial mortgage lender's office—the important thing for the reader is the practical application of what the company and people at that scene are doing. What process could the reader copy? What material could the reader use? Which techniques might be worse to use and which better? What has the owner, manager, worker learned that the reader should learn as well?

To my mind, the distinctions between case histories, site visits, project reports and company profiles blur quite easily. In fact, you should be careful as you approach trade magazine editors to write these stories because the jargon, so to speak, isn't really set in stone. The terminology of the first three types is used interchangeably, and I'm putting definition to them here simply for the purpose of delineating what I understand to be the differences.

Case histories

Case histories go right to the heart of the trade editor's impulse toward practical applications. In the case history, you basically shows the facts of a process and what results the process has yielded. In a few magazines, editors allow the reader to draw their own conclusions from a Jack Webb-like "just the facts, ma'am" approach, but most magazines, I've found, like the writer to suggest at least some preliminary evaluation of the success or failure of the case.

With case histories, you should do some research on the background leading up to the project you are reporting on. Generally this means interviewing the principle players in the particular project. For a case history, say, on a construction project, you would interview the architect, the general contractor, and possibly the owner or one of the most important consulting designers. On a chain-wide retail promotion, you might interview the product buyer, the merchandising vice president, and perhaps the corporate head of the display department.

Site visits. Site visits differ from case histories not so much in the approach to the information as much as the parties interviewed. In case histories, you generally interview the people at the top; on site visits, you include the people in the middle or lower as well. Remember the pyramid of information. Site visits concentrate on the broad base of that information. On a construction project, for instance, you might interview the project superintendent, the mechanical subcontractor, the crane operator, the framing foreman—you get down into the crafts-man level. For a retail site visit, you go to one of the store in the chain that's doing the merchandising promotion, talk to the person who set up the display and the store manager to see how the display is working.

Project reports. A project report is somewhere between the first two types of articles. You want to present facts, you want to interview the principles, but you also want to go into the field and get the reaction of the worker who is there on a daily basis. In short, you gear your interviews from the top of the information pyramid to near the bottom, and then your report synthesizes these reactions to reach an evaluation.

Company Profiles. Company profiles can be the easiest or the most difficult pieces that you write. The reason I list them here with other "on the scene" stories is because, in a very real sense, they will be one of the three types: a case history, a site visit, or a project report.

Company profiles are some of the most ticklish stories to write because of the sometimes contending motivations of company officers, magazine editors, and magazine salesmen.

Company officers, naturally, will want such a profile to put the best face on the company's endeavors and manage-ment, usually with an eye toward attracting more customers. In magazines where profiles are not part of the normal edito-rial mix but are a separate function altogether—often shown physically by being a special insert in the magazine—the ac-tual editorial staff may have little or no control over material that goes into the profile. The magazine's ad sales staff will want to please the company being profiled, and seldom if ever complain that the profile is essentially "puff" public relations.

In magazines where such a profile is a normal part of the editorial mix, editors still must walk a fine line between presenting a story of substance without a pro or con bias based on facts, and dealing with the ongoing slogan of the advertising sales division that advertising is the engine which pulls the magazine's train so editorial shouldn't be allowed to tamper with the fuel (i.e., present a negative profile).

As a writer, you can often find yourself caught between these competing camps. These are the kinds of stories where you must understand your own motivations. Do you need a paycheck? Do you need a way to break into the magazine stable? Do you dare write a "puff" profile to the specifications of the advertising department or the target company and take a risk that the editorial staff will brand you as a lightweight who isn't fit to write any of the regular editorial product? These are the questions you must answer for yourself on a case by case basis.

Structures that work

If there is one subject that writing manuals seem to love, it is structure. So many wonderful guides exist that I hesitate to even offer my own puny comments, but in case you might want to hear just one more opinion, here it is.

Structure, I think, is guided more by the length of your assignment than by any other factor. I don't intend to catalog all the structures possible for a trade magazine story; instead I'll offer two that I have found to work 99 percent of the time for most trade magazines.

Pyramid structure. Pyramid structure is been the traditional structure for news stories. In the pyramid structure, you basically tell what happened to whom, when and where, and then continue to broaden the story with some appropriate how and embellish with other appropriate who, what, when, where and why facts.

With the pyramid structure, once you tag what happened to whom, etc., at the beginning of the piece, as long as every fact in the following paragraphs relate back in some way to the opening event, you can generally present the material in whatever order you want. The structure is called a pyramid because you are starting at a single point and expand from there with no bias.

In reality, the way you order your facts has its own sort of rhetoric, its own sort of persuasiveness, and pyramid structure in the hands of a master can be as intricate and deft as any other type of structure you care to think of.

What I will suggest here, though, is that pyramid structure is best suited—in trade magazine use—to stories of less than five hundred words. The thrust of pyramid structure is to present the facts as quickly and fully as possible with little or no commentary. In a short piece, the facts will pull the reader along better than any embellishment, especially if the single-point event that began the piece interests them in the first place.

The pyramid structure simplifies your self-editing process. You mainly have to worry about spelling names and places correctly, and you must check your facts to be sure they are accurate. The pyramid structure isn't designed for great literature; it's designed to spit out as many facts as possible in the shortest amount of space.

That's also the drawback to this structure: Related details can be scattered and correlations unfocused which means you are asking the reader to do much of the work. Also, pyramid structure has little in the way of "suspense," a time-honored strategy for getting a reader to finish the entire piece.

Chapter structure. Most pieces longer than 500 words should use some form of "chapter" structure. The name means just what it says: you divide the elements of the story up into manageable groups known as chapters. For a 600-word piece, maybe you have 3 chapters of 150 words plus a 75-word lead and 75-word close. There are no set rules for how many words go into a chapter, the determination comes from the subject itself.

Most topics will naturally break down into a variety of subtopics. In a construction company profile, for example, the most natural breakdown is where a company has come from (its history), where it is now (what projects the company is currently working on) and where it is going (what markets will it approach in the future).

On longer pieces, chapter divisions are often shown by subheads or even subtitles for each chapter with subheads within the chapter. On shorter pieces, chapter divisions may not be shown at all. The main thing to remember is that chapters are simply a tool to organize material for the reader so that one area can be covered before going on to the next without confusion.

Chapter structure works well with a variety of presentation strategies—comparison and contrast, cause and effect, time, space, and parallels—which make up the rhetorical method of most trade feature articles. These are long-standing devices of rhetoric, but it is worthwhile to revisit the mechanics involved in these important structures.

Comparison/contrast. As the name implies, in this structure you compare two similar things with each other, or show how they contrast, or often both. There really are only two basic ways to go about this. First, make sure you are going apples to apples and oranges to oranges, but not apples to oranges.

For instance, if you were comparing two different buildings, you could compare building A's exterior walls to building B's, then the roof of A to the roof of B, then A's foundation to B's foundation, etc. The structure, if diagrammed, would look something like:

A1 (exterior walls)   —   B1 (exterior walls)
A2 (roof)   —   B2 (roof)
A3 (foundation)   —   B3 (foundation)

Apples to apples.

The other option is to look first at the elements of A as a whole, then at the elements of B as a whole. Again, though, good structure and style means that you follow the same order within each section, i.e.:

A1 (exterior walls)
A2 (roof)

A3 (foundation), then:
B1 (exterior walls)
B2 (roof)
B3 (foundation)

As a general rule of thumb, the second strategy works best with shorter pieces, the first strategy is often less confusing in a longer piece. The main thing is to make sure your reader can make the logical jump with you easily. If they can't, they'll stop reading.

Time or space presentations should also be broken up into chapters. If you are doing a story, say, on the layout of a store, go in a logical spatial sequence. This can be done with larger stores by taking the reader on a trek from one department to the next, then from the first floor to the second, front to back, left to right. The main thing to remember is to keep the reader's sense of spatial movement sequential. Don't jump from a department on the first floor to a new department on the second, then to the loading dock on the first floor, then back to another department across the building and up on the second floor.

Time, too, often offers a logical sequence. Be careful trying to break up a chronology. The clearest choices are to move sequentially from beginning to end, or to start at the end and move sequentially from the end back to the beginning. If you are describing a baking process, for instance, you can most easily move from the process of mixing the batter through the various steps to the finished, wrapped product.

Parallel constructions are also a staple of trade magazine structures. Pro and con. Cause and effect. Problem and solution. But again, remember to keep them straight for the reader. Problem A should go with solution A. Pro argument A should go with con response A, pro argument B with con response B, and so forth. Cause A with effect A, etc.

You can also reverse the approach for affect, putting solution A followed by problem A that it solved, or what effect A was and what cause A was. If the effect had more than one cause, you should put all the causes together then explain the effect (or effects) before moving on to the next set.

From the standpoint of logical structure, it was interesting to listen to the debate and presentations on the Clinton impeachment in both the House and the Senate. Every effort seemed to be made, on both sides of the aisle, to argue apples to oranges, peaches to potatoes, and barley to beans.

If the American public didn't seem to "get it," the reason just may have been that our legislators were consciously trying to compare A to 12, not A to A or even A to B. When you can't directly make a comparison, you are actually making an analogy. Analogies, we understand at a subconscious level, are essentially metaphors and valid only insofar as we accept the metaphor. Few people are fooled very long by such an approach, and such a strategy simply kills any credibility on the part of the speaker—or the writer—if the metaphor isn't accepted. Perhaps that's why so many were unimpressed with the arguments on either side and why most Americans, according to polls taken, were paying little or no attention to such a momentous proceeding.

As a former editor, I would say the number one problem I have seen in most freelance articles was simply the failure to adopt and carry through on these simple structural strategies. The strategies work, at the most basic level, because they create a sense of tension, a sense of suspense, that pulls the reader through the article. Here's the problem; here's how it was solved. Here's how we were delayed starting, here's how we made up the time in the middle of the project, and here's how we breathlessly finished ahead of schedule.

I would submit to you that these basic strategies—rhetorical devices that have come down to us from before Aristotle—work as strategies for writing because they present as much a sense of drama as of logic. We read the headline and it promises an answer to a question we've been pondering. Our curiosity is intrigued first by the topic sentence that promises our quest will be fulfilled, and then one by one, the pieces of the answer are explained until we are compelled to slog on through the miasma of words on a straight path of ideas until our quest for understanding is fulfilled by the end of the article.

It ain't Shakespeare, but it is higher drama than reading the washing machine repair manual.

Finding a story

Now that you know a bit about organizing such stories, you next have to go out and find a story to write. James Joseph, a former chairman of the ASJA's Southern California Chapter and a prolific business writer, tells about his early days as a freelance trade magazine writer in *The Complete Guide to Writing Nonfiction*. He recounts that he would stop in at the local newspaper office in a small town, tell the editor he was looking for a good business story, and in almost every case would be given a usable lead. Joseph notes that he wrote one story per day seven days a week during that time in his life.

Duane Newcomb, also a prolific trade freelancer who had a background in retail, recalls that he would start at one end of a mall, walk through, interview several store managers and snap a couple of photos, and walk out the other end of the mall with seven or eight stories to sell.

My own experience is similar, but different. Since I concentrate primarily on the construction industry, if I'm out of material I simply get in the car and drive around town. Fortunately, since I live in a growing metro area in a region often overlooked by national trade magazines, it isn't difficult to come up with several good leads from an afternoon's drive.

The point is, you will have to match your technique to your own region's resources and your own sense of initiative. Joseph's notion of beginning with community newspaper editors is a sound one, whether you live in a large metro area or out in the country. Your best bet, though, is to begin with industries that you know, or with people that you know in a particular industry. Friends, relatives, neighbors, chance acquaintances—all can be sources of good leads.

The best leads for your next story, though, often come from the person you are interviewing for a current story.

Chances are they will know the local industry intimately and can point you toward several people who have an interesting tale to tell.

There's really no substitute for networking. Good trade stories, like any story, begin with people and follow with facts. So canvass your friends and neighbors. Ask what they do and who they work with.

Getting to know an industry

One of the best aspects of "on the scene" stories is that they force you to immerse yourself in what an industry does, and more specifically, the language it speaks.

Every industry has terms either specific to the industry or words that change meaning or at least shades of meaning from industry to industry. Your first effort in any industry is to learn the names of things.

Learning a name implies learning the slang name as well. Acronyms abound in every industry, especially in the names of companies. If you want to write a construction story, for example, your first contact may suggest that you phone the E.D. of AGC to find out about large projects in the state. It's not too difficult to figure out that E.D. is executive director once you understand that AGC stands for Associated General Contractors which has at least one chapter in every state in the U.S.

When it comes to getting down the names of "things" within an industry, there are no stupid questions. If you don't know what a "broken back beam" is, you can't do a story about below-grade sports arenas (and you better know that "below-grade" in this instance does not mean substandard, it means below normal ground level).

Another area where you must learn the language of the industry is in how the industry specifies its working elements. These specifications can cover a wide range. In designing audio/visual systems, for example, all specifications in the design are going to be built around the "signal frequency" maximums. Put as simply as possible, if the engineer is designing the system to include computer presentations, he will have to design switching systems and specify equipment that can handle higher frequency signals (and hence cost more). If he is designing the system to handle only video and audio signals, the switching systems can handle lower frequency gear that's less expensive.

Categories are other words you will need to become familiar with. An ISO 9000 company has a significant edge over a non-ISO company in exporting to many foreign companies. You'd better find out why. In construction, a heavy/highway contractor is worlds different from a commercial building contractor and a commercial building contractor is worlds away from a residential spec home builder.

Common sense won't always tell you the distinction. I've discovered, for instance, that in some industries a "business development manager" is a different category from a "marketing manager" and in some industries, the term is virtually interchangeable.

Measures are another area where you must learn a least the rudiments to write an intelligible story. Medicine uses the metric system; construction still uses feet, yards, and cubic yards unless it is a government project or otherwise is mandated to use metric. Would you know what a "square" is if you were figuring masonry block or asphalt shingles?

You'll also have to learn, in addition, the general language of business. What's the difference between payables and receivables? What's the difference between a bond and a stock? A "C" corporation and an "S" corporation? A joint venture and a partnership? If you don't know, find out, either by asking or by consulting a good general business book.

Find a mentor. As you begin to look for stories to write, you'll discover that most people—though certainly not all—are willing to help. One of the true advantages trade journalism has over the mainstream variety is that most businesses are excited to think they will get some exposure about the good things they can do.

The on the scene article will put you in touch with what is

going on "in the trenches." You will discover individuals who have a wealth of practical knowledge that will both help inform your writing and increase your interest. One of the criticisms I have heard about trade journalism is how boring it is to write about business procedures and techniques. But boredom is in the eye of the beholder.

My experience with construction is a good example. I don't have an extensive background in the field. I do have a compulsion, however, to make something useful or entertaining or enlightening where nothing existed before. Hence I have always been a compulsive writer, even when I had a job doing something else, which I did for a full decade.

Imagine my surprise when I discovered that same compulsion in the field of construction, the compulsion to make something where nothing existed before. Writers write, I've discovered, because they must. Builders build, I've also learned, because they must. It's compulsive. It's really their favorite pastime. Doctors doctor because they must. Programmers program because they enjoy it.

These impulses exist at all levels from the field worker to the manager. That's not to say that many people are not doing exactly what they want to do. It is to say, however, that when you discover your interviewee is turned on by what they do, you will be energized yourself.

And what is more important for your future as a trade writer, you'll discover people who are passionate about what they do almost always want to share their excitement, want to help inform you so you can understand why their job is so fulfilling. These will be your mentors in the trade. Treasure them.

So get out in the field. That's where the excitement is.

Chapter 7

How to write how-to and service stories that sell.

If "on-the-scene" stories are one staple of trade magazines, how-to and service stories are the other. That's good news for freelancers because the two story types are among the easiest to research, to write, and to sell.

What is the basic difference between a how-to and a service story? Personally I find the difference is a combination of presentation technique and intended outcome, but the research needed is often the same. From the standpoint of cost-effectiveness, that means I can almost always develop two stories to sell for the expense of one.

How-to stories

How to stories give specific step-by-step directions on how to reach a particular objectives. They roughly follow five different forms:

1. **Step-by-step**. In one sense, all how-to stories are step by step. To be effective as a how-to, you must tell the reader how to accomplish a specific task or reach a specific goal, and if you are being honest with the reader, you will describe every

step that it takes to reach the goal.

However, most step-by-step articles focus just on the steps with only a brief mention of the goal's desirability in the lead and a repetition of this motivation at the conclusion. Step-by-step stories concentrate on the nuts and bolts of getting a task done, often with little or no explanation of why each step is necessary. I would say this type of article is found most often when the goal is specifically functional, such as installing a ceramic tile, developing a payables monitoring program, or even the procedure for coming up with a business mission statement.

2. **The "recovery" or "self-help" article.** The archetype of this article is found extensively in women's general interest magazines such as *Family Circle* or *Woman's Day*, with titles such as "How I Saved the Family Vacation", "Saving Yourself From Addition: One Woman's Story," etc.

If the step-by-step story concentrates on the nuts and bolts, the recovery article concentrates on why you are turning the screwdriver and holding the wrench. In other words, the focus is as much on how to motivate yourself or your workers at each step as it is on what the step is.

3. **The evolutionary story.** I like to think of the evolutionary story as an extended analogy. In this type of story, you are still showing the reader how to reach a goal, but you do so by reporting the stages that a real-life company or individual went through in achieving the goal. Often the "on the scene" story takes this form when you weave in a backstory of preceding information, but an evolutionary story can also be done without going on the site for the reader. Many business analysis stories take this form. Essentially, you tell your reader that the subject reached a desirable goal (higher profit margins, better employee relations, reduced inventory, etc.) and let the subject outline the steps for your reader.

One element that sets the evolutionary story apart from the step-by-step is the opportunity to have the subject share their motivations and their own assessment of the results achieved. Was it worth it? Would they do it differently the next time? What could be done better?

4. **The component-based story.** Not every goal can be reached with a simple step-by-step process. A good example is the continuing saga of social security. As I write, two similar but different proposals are being considered to make Social Security funding viable until 2055. However, regardless of which proposal technique is chosen, other components—a healthy stock market, a dollar that holds value, a lack of catastrophic world events, freedom from a national or global economic depression, a consensus that politics wouldn't eventually try to control the stock market, and even the absence of a comet striking the earth—will also be very key factors on whether either proposal can succeed.

Business faces a wide range of challenges every day, so often a business goal must consider a number of component goals to be reached for the overall goal to be successful. If you want to open a new market, for instance, one component is to do a better job of advertising and publicity in that market to get brand or name recognition. Another goal is to develop solid distribution capability to serve that market. Another component is to realign your fiscal budgets to reflect the actual costs of business and potential profits in such a market. Still another may be finding new sources of supply to maintain your expanded production. A company may even need to change its corporate culture to be acceptable in this new market. And to break in successfully, all of these separate components must work together.

The component story looks at how each of these factors can be achieved, citing the steps that must be taken within each area to be successful. Where this story differs from the more straightforward step-by-step article is in the scope of the goal to be achieved. In the step-by-step story, you tell how to install ceramic tile around the bathtub; in the component story, you tell how a commercial flooring contractor can successfully move into the bathroom remodeling marketplace.

5. **The exercise-based story.** The last type of how-to story is not seen as much in the trade magazine arena as it is in the consumer field. And that's good news for freelancers who have a turn for puzzles and education. A straw poll I conducted among several editors cutting across different industries is instructive: only one had ever had such an article offered to them. Depending on the quality of the piece, though, almost all of them thought it would be interesting to run an industry quiz or puzzle. If you have a talent for such a piece, give it a try.

Service stories

Service stories outline a problem or goal, not telling you what to do generally, but where to find someone or something to solve your problem. It can also suggest ways the problem has been solved by others in a general way. The most basic difference that I see between the service story and the how-to is the lack of specific steps and suggestions being given to solve the problem.

Service stories often take the form of an informal survey where a basic question is posed and the responses give the reader insight into how others are dealing with the problem or how his own method stacks up against "current practice."

In fact, service stories taking this approach can sometimes lead into more cutting edge investigative journalism. I recall a story several years ago that asked a number of subcontractors whether bid shopping was a modern problem in the construction industry's bidding practices. The can of worms opened at both ends as frustrated subcontractors vented their frustration at giving a general contractor a low bid only to have the general "shop" the bid—calling other subs and asking if they could beat the price. As it turned out, owners were doing it to the general contractors as well, and the subcontractors were doing it to their sub-tier subcontractors. What began as a simple service story question, "How Do You Protect Yourself Against Bid Shopping?" became a report on the depths of skullduggery in the region's construction industry.

Information only. A separate type of service story is an "information please" story, often telling the reader about specific products or services in the market, sometimes with a comparison and analysis, but more often without. An example would be a story that lists new products and tells about their various individual specifications, but offers no judgment or criticism on their ability to perform as advertised.

Most non-comparison stories are done in-house. Trade magazines, I've found, are generally deluged with product press releases, so this is a good way to make use of them. At some trades, however, product producers have to pay for the space just as they would for an advertisement.

Most trade magazines, however, do not have the staffing or the expertise to conduct product comparison testing a la *Consumer Reports.* If you are a backhoe operator who has worked with the newest Caterpillar and the newest Kobelco, a comparison of their performance might be a good article to offer. This is virtually an untapped field in some trade magazine industries, but one that offers tremendous potential for a freelancer whose background, training, and understanding qualify to make an informed judgement between two or more similar products in a given field.

Write in chapters

Chapter construction not only works well in how-to and service stories, it's practically mandatory.

How-to stories generally have a four-part structure:

The Preview—what the reader can learn. This is your "hook." Two tactics work well here. You can begin your article by describing a set of problematic circumstances the reader is familiar with, or you can begin with an anecdote about a specific company or person experiencing a *problem* the reader is familiar with. The main goal is to get the reader nodding his head and mentally saying, "Yes, that's exactly what I've been having trouble with."

The Notification—what advice you plan to give. This is a simple two-part formulaic sentence sketching the goal to be achieved and how many steps it will take to reach.

The Steps—what the reader must do first, second, third, fourth and so on to reach the goal.

The Motivator—an optional ending that recaps the importance of the goal, reminds the reader he has been shown how to reach the goal, and urges the reader not to procrastinate in beginning the process. I find the motivator paragraph is too heavy a treatment for shorter how-to pieces which I prefer to end simply with the last step. On longer articles, however, the motivator paragraph is a good opportunity to remind the reader what each step was, why it is necessary, and that the goal can be accomplished.

With this four-part structure, it's easy to see that step-by-step information will break into natural chapters, especially on longer articles. In a how-to article, chapter "steps" should be announced by subheads. To pull the reader through the article, put the reader into these subheads:

With commandments—*Write in chapters.*
With fulfillments—*Doubling and tripling your sales.*
With explanations—*Finish by editing out repetitive words.*

Where to find how-to and service story ideas

The short answer is: everywhere. I said earlier that I love these kinds of stories because they offer a two-for-one on research time. Sometimes they offer a three-, four-, or five-for-one. Let's put that notion into a more concrete form. In fact, let's use concrete forms.

General topic—The below-grade addition to the Marriott Library at the University of Utah. An on-the-scene story.

How-to—"How to use plain wood forms to decorate concrete."

"How to calculate concrete load-bearing capability for below-grade foundation replacements."

"How to schedule concrete deliveries on limited access sites to minimize delivery charges."

"How universities can add space by building down instead of up."

Service—"The 12 top admixtures for worry free decorative concrete."

"New restaurant equipment cuts utility bills and installation time."

"New interactive software for MRIs improve resolution."

"A/E/C Expo unveils integrated CAD and project budgeting software."

Self-help—"Keeping chaos out of product development."

"Measure your performance."

"When your partner doesn't pull his weight . . ."

Chapters for service stories group related chunks of information. Tell where to get the material, how much material is needed for various applications, the approximate cost of the material and other necessary details.

Service stories must be as specific as possible wherever possible (prices vary by region, how long it takes to ship, etc.). If there was ever a true Jack Webb "just-the-facts-ma'am," it's in the service story.

Remember, too, that some readers understand by reading, some by seeing, and most by a combination. If there is one complaint I have consistently heard from editors, it's that freelance service stories are seldom well illustrated. Look beyond the photo of the main expert who helped forward your research on the piece, and if you are going to do an opinion round-up, for example, at a convention, get photos of the people you are surveying.

Conclude your story by reminding the reader of the benefits of reaching the goal or following your advice.

Self-help articles

Self-help articles differ from simpler how-to articles because they typically are not about fixing a physical problem so much as a situational or personal problem. Because situations are more complex to fix, the simple step-by-step approach—still valid in many situations—may be too simplified for the self-help piece.

Self-help articles more often present "chunks" of different topical information for the reader to consider. Although self-help articles follow a simple formula, don't be fooled into thinking there is no room for creativity:

1. Start with a statement of the problem to solve.

2. Talk about the causes of the problem, and as you go through the writing, provide solid information backed up by expert opinion.

3. Give five or more suggestions from the experts on how to cure the problem.

4. Close the article by reminding the reader of the benefits derived from solving the problem.

This is a simple, but powerful, formula in the hands of a skilled writer. Detailed analysis and the choice of quotations can determine whether this type of article is a turkey or an award-winner.

The "information please" article is also formulaic, generally done best as a list. A good lead for this article is to describe a common industry situation the reader can relate to, such as the difficulty of finding information on the most desirable qualities of different widgets. The article then lists the various places where such information is available and how those information sources differ in presenting the information. This kind of "information please" form is a staple in the Internet reference books that have exploded into the book market in the last few years. While they are easy and quick to write once the research is done, the "information please" article is often the most time-consuming to research.

With the "information please" article, you must carefully consider your potential investment in time before you agree to the assignment. My own rule of thumb is to figure that such an article takes five times the research time of a standard project profile, so it is seldom that I will accept such an assignment. On the other hand, if you already completed the majority of the research while you were working on another project, it can be an additional boon to your pocketbook. I write a short "information please" online newsletter, which still consumes much more time than a typical article, but I am doing most of the research about sites for other reasons, so it makes financial sense to re-use that research in a separate piece.

Remember: The challenge of how-to and service articles is three-fold. First, and especially with the how-to article, you must make sure the article delivers on its promise. If you haven't taught the reader what you promised to teach by the end of the article, you must revise and expand the article until you have.

Second, your article has an implied promise that it will teach them a way of doing things they weren't aware of. Don't disappoint with generalities. If you promise to show them how to improve their profit margin by a percentage point, don't just tell them to lower their production cost half a percent and raise their price half a percent. You *can* tell, them, however, several specific ways to reduce production costs to reach that half percent and specific ways to reconfigure their accounting, sales, and promotion procedures to make a half-percent price hike palatable to their existing customers.

Third, make sure your directions are understandable, easy to follow, and succinct. Sometimes you discover that you are trying to cram two article subjects into one. As you write, if you find that a given step takes several extra paragraphs more than any other step, that's a signal you really have two articles, not one.

So sell both.

Chapter 8.

Writing round-up, trend, and show stories for the trades.

Another staple of both general and trade magazines is the round-up story where you herd your experts' opinions together into a single issue "pen." It's a story that seems easy to do on the surface—after all, the only real work involved is to call up five or six experts, ask them their opinion on a certain subject, and then write down their answers.

Anybody could do that, though. I'm sure you've seen the Q & A articles where the interviewee's name is in bold followed by a colon and then there are a few paragraphs quoting them directly.

Next comes the second interviewee and so on and so forth. Sometimes, when this approach is used, the article is called a "roundtable." Most of the work in these is editing, not writing, so you seldom find yourself doing this type of assignment because it is more the job of the magazine's editor.

Round-ups, however, must be written to be effective. Yes, you must discover a topic to be covered, and then you must interview several experts to get their opinion on the subject, but if all you do is quote them directly with only a modicum of editing, you've probably missed the point of the round-up article. The goal for the writer, according to Gary Provost in the *Handbook of Magazine Article Writing*, is to turn a survey into interesting reading.

The most interesting reading in trade magazines, I believe, is an *argument*.

Everybody likes a good argument. Look how fascinated we are as a nation with the quibbling between lawyers during a trial and the give and take of politicians when they are running for office and even after they are in. And let's not forget a good football, basketball, or baseball game, or even a swim meet and a ping pong tournament. After all, sports are simply highly ritualized arguments that "I'm better than you, and the tribe I hang around with is better than your tribe."

Honestly, most editors can't get enough of this stuff because arguments are interesting. We feel ourselves pulled into the article as we read and as we begin to identify more and more with one side or the other. As we get deeper and deeper into the discussion, we decide which tribe we belong to—and it is always the one that's right!

Or we can, as readers, go the extreme opposite: Every expert quoted in this article has a head full of wool and marbles. Nothing they say bears any resemblance to the truth. Only my opinion considers the full range of factors on this topic and synthesizes those factors into a cohesive and workable viewpoint. (Next stop: Letter to the editor.)

The point Provost makes—and I think it is an important point—is that the round-up article must be *written* or it is only a survey. The problem with a survey, you see, is that you can't argue with its conclusions directly. In fact, what ends up happening with a survey is that most of the argumentation centers on the validity of the survey method (since the somewhat false assumption is that if the method is faulty, the finding of the survey is faulty as well), but when 90 percent of the people say the President was a schmuck, all you can argue is the validity of the polling method, not the fact that 90 percent of whomever was polled, and in whatever way, actually said the guy was a schmuck.

A second reason that round-up articles are popular is because they are the written equivalent of town meetings. Let's say that you haven't formed your opinion yet as a reader. The round-up article can help you see the various points of view on the issue and help you make an informed decision.

Education is one of the main reasons why we attend a town meeting isn't it? After all, we need to know why we oppose the building of a new shopping center on the property adjoining the village park.

From the writer's point of view, round-up and trend articles are a never-ending source of topics, the raw materials that drive your career. Take an example from the general media. During the Clinton impeachment proceedings, it was all you could do to avoid a round-up show on television or radio, or a round-up story in any weekly news magazine, daily paper, or shock tabloid. But when you took a closer look, few of these venues were offering any "news" in the sense of actually having a newsworthy item.

But look at the popularity of this format. Sometimes I think it must go back to our days in the caves. With nothing else to do at night, cave people may have sat around arguing the merits of the wooly mammoth that was driven into the pit that day. Perhaps the meat was tastier than the last mastodon, says one. Nope, this is by far the tastiest mammoth in years, says another, and the entertainment is on.

Arguments educate us in a unique way by stretching our imagination. Perhaps we had never thought of this or that particular drawback. Perhaps one of the quotations makes the little light bulb of a new idea go on in our head. Perhaps we just enjoy the verbal dexterity of dueling proponents.

Perhaps we have secretly caught on to a trend ourselves, and then are delighted to see in a round-up that only one other source has caught on as well which means we'll be ahead in the race to take advantage of this trend.

Whatever the reason, round-up and trend stories provide a broad crop of material ready for harvest.

Writing the round-up story

Round-up stories, trend stories, and even to some extent show stories, essentially start as surveys. The survey can be more or less formal, depending on the circumstance and the particular slant you are looking for. Make no mistake, however, you must start from a particular slant just as you would with any other story to give yourself a guideline to proceed.

Published surveys of one sort or another often can provide inspiration. Where do you find information about surveys in the industry you want to write about? From the experts in that industry, including the trade magazines and especially the associations that cover the industry.

Associations are a great place to begin research for most any round-up or trend topic. In chapter four we mentioned the Gale's Directory. For the serious trade writer, it's almost imperative to contact the media relations directory of the pertinent industries you plan to cover, let them know that you are a writer covering the industry for a variety of magazines, and ask to be put on their press release list. But be prepared . . . .

As you become known to these associations, you are going to find yourself with a constant stream of mail that has to be sorted through and filed so you can retrieve it. As a practical matter, I suggest you talk to some of your local industry contacts to discover which associations are important and which are marginal to your needs. For example, in covering the construction industry, I've developed good working relations with most of the major industry associations, but I've never really developed a relationship with the Painting and Decorating Contractors Association (PDCA) for the simple reason that I almost never write a story concerning painting. I do, however, do many stories on decorating, but find that the International Interior Design Association (IIDA) is a better source of information for me. If I were writing much about paint or coatings, however, and less about the choice of materials in an interior design, then the PDCA would move to the forefront and the IIDA would probably be less important to my needs.

As part of fulfilling their mission to members, associations often initiate surveys on topics important to their members. Sometimes the survey results are available, sometimes they are not publicly circulated but is available only to members. When this is true, though, you can often get a copy of the survey from a member that you know.

Another good service that an association's media relations director can do is point you toward experts you can interview. Generally I contact the media relations coordinator at the association, outline what ground I need to cover for the article, and ask their advice about who to contact. It's also a good idea to specify what kind of magazine audience you are writing for, if not a particular magazine. Writing a broad round-up for a national magazine, for instance, generally requires getting the opinion of experts from across the country. If I am writing for a regional audience, however, I'll normally seek out experts within the region, with maybe one interview from a nationally recognized expert to set up the national events that have led up to the debate.

Experts also can point you to a significant or recent survey. Why stress starting with a completed survey rather than coming up with one on your own?

Surveys rarely happen in a vacuum. Surveys usually result from two important business impulses: 1) A sudden hiccup in the smooth functioning of an industry, or 2) ongoing situations can either menace or embolden an industry's profitability and therefore its survival. Situation 1 makes good fodder for a round-up; situation 2 fuels the trend story, but can be the basis of a round-up story as well. With situation 1, naturally, one of the questions to be asked is whether the situation is the start of a trend.

Getting started on the trend story

Although published surveys or unpublished surveys conducted by industry experts are one place to start, remember that you are going to cover the ground again with your own personal survey. If you can detect a trend or a potentially volatile topic before an industry expert does, you may be in an even stronger position to pitch the story to a trade magazine editor.

One of the strong trends in the construction industry over the past ten years has been a change in the way projects are delivered. Larger commercial building contractors have moved away from the tradition of bidding on a building after the architect has designed it for an owner. Owners have been commissioning the contractors directly, and then the contractor hires the architect to design the building. This has changed the dynamics of the process in very significant ways. In the old scheme, the architect essentially was the owner's representative whenever a dispute would come up. In the new system, with the architect working for the contractor, that relationship is diminished.

That's not news, though. What is news, however, is how this change in delivering building projects is affecting the way contractors hire management. Under the old tradition, a contractor needed a project manager who had combined the discipline and "my way or the highway" attitude of a marine drill sergeant with the mathematical acumen of a CPA. With design/build, however, project managers need interpersonal skills to build teams to get the project done, plus the mathematical acumen of a CPA, plus the scheduling skills of an air traffic controller.

That's led to major changes in the education, cultivation, and hiring of project managers, and it has left the old-school project managers in jeopardy. So the round-up topic became: Is there any place left for the tough project manager. (Answer: only in highway construction where every project is bid, but even that arena is undergoing change.)

For the freelancer, this is an important lesson. What started out as a broad trend every construction magazine was reporting on led to a specific effect that could be turned into a credible and important article. The broad implications are written and rewritten in round-up articles by magazine staff. To crack a market, you must come up with an unseen implication.

How many sources?

Determining how many sources you need is both simple and difficult. On the surface, it's easy to predict you will need to interview a minimum of three, but probably will end up using no more than five. Seldom will you see an article quoting more than five people unless it is a roundtable "transcript" that we described in the opening part of the chapter.

Before you run out to find three to five people to interview, however, take a moment to assess what you need to make the article work. The often unspoken goal of a round-up is to reach a conclusion, however tentative.

Yes, that's biased reporting, but as I said earlier, everything you write is an argument. At least with a round-up, folks get to vote.

Which is why three or five is so much more appealing than interviewing four. But it's your article. When you have the odd number, though, you will reach a majority decision (which hopefully you put in either your concluding paragraph or just before it.) An even number of interviews, however, can be effective as well in showing how much an industry is polarized by an issue. To take a more recent example, think back to the talk show discussions during the Clinton impeachment proceedings. I personally don't believe there was more than two or three of the hundred or so shows I watched that didn't balance the number of conservatives with the number of liberals, the number of Republicans with the number of Democrats, or the number of congressional members of the House and Senate with the number of press aides from the White House.

The net effect, then, was to show the nation how polarizing the experience was. How different would the effect have been if the panels were loaded with a majority from one side or another?

On the other hand, even when you interview an odd number of experts or industry members, it is still a good idea to reach for some kind of balance depending on the issue. You need, in many industries, both a female and a male opinion, and maybe pro and con within each industry. If you are covering an industry with unequal gender representation, you should at the least try to strike an ethnic balance. Sometimes it can be difficult. When I first began as an editor in the construction industry, it was very difficult to find a female construction company owner, and almost impossible in Utah to find a minority owner, although the ones you did find tended to be exceptionally good at what they did. Fortunately the situation improved greatly during my tenure.

But there are other ways to have imbalance. Try finding a hot Internet entrepreneur over the age of 50. Try finding a bed-and-breakfast owner under the age of 35. Try finding a black bicycle racing shop owner in the U.S. Try finding a white rapper who's any good. Is this stereotyping?

Perhaps, but in many industries it is also a current reality. One thing is certain: no stereotype lasts forever in the modern world. In fact, I'll bet that the number of over-50 Internet entrepreneurs triples by the year 2025. I have a less enthusiastic prediction for white rappers. What do you think?

Organize the story

Round-up and trend stories are among the easiest stories to organize. The trend, after all, is the slant of the story but not necessarily the lead. Think of a trend as a hypothesis that you are going to explore with the reader. As you get ready to develop the research for the story, you can use the old high school debate formula to set up the hypothesis for yourself: Resolved: Bid shopping is a disappearing form of coercion in the construction industry. Resolved: LFA-1 molecules on killer T cells hold the cure for the common cold. Resolved: Downsizing at major telecommunications corporations is fueling a rise of small, competitive start-up companies in the industry.

Your hypothesis, however, doesn't always make for a good lead. It can be used though in a type of lead called a "startling assertion":

In the fall of 1992 John Smith was laid off from Multinational Telecomm as part of a general restructuring of the com-

128

pany. Left to his own devices, Smith developed a new widget that routes twisted copper-pair connections 1000 times faster than the old industry standard. Recently he negotiated a deal with Multinational which will pay him 100 times what he was making at his old job. His story isn't unique in the fast-changing telecommunications industry."

Often round-up and trend stories use material that is scattered across time, or perhaps across geography. The bullet lead (also known as the round-up lead) effectively organizes far-flung material to jump into a trend. This lead is usually a two-parter. The first part is a collage of facts; the second part, a general statement of the situation. For example:

"Hotzman General Contractors, Dusseldorf, has bid on fewer than three projects in the last two years. Spandel Construction, New York, recently purchased High-Wire Architecture of Philadelphia as one of their operating units. Wholesome Contracting, Salt Lake City, Utah, has entered into a joint venture with Moral General Contractors and Practical Architectural Associates, both of Ogden, to perform a multi-phase project that will last for four years. All of the joint venture partners will avoid bidding on projects during that time."

Why have these firms moved away from the traditional hard-bid process of commercial construction? Because they believe that long-term repeat customers who work exclusively with their firm is the wave of the future in construction.

The second paragraph of this lead is the general statement, the hypothesis you will be proving (or disproving) in the body of your story. The format is simple, but works on almost any type of round-up, trend, or show story. Another example:

Joe Buck is just 21 and fresh out of college. Phil Smith is 85 years old and newly retired from his company. Tom Jones is 50 and has just been named president of the company he has worked for the past 20 years. They met each other for the first time last month in Las Vegas and each learned something new from the other.

That's just one of the results of the annual World of Concrete held in Vegas each January. It's a chance to meet colleagues with new ideas as well as see a tremendous amount of innovative equipment for the concrete industry.

Once you have your lead, the round-up and trend stories generally take the same organizational shape:

• Describe the trend you've discovered or summarize the state of the situation as it exists (for the round-up). You can do this directly, but a better tactic is to have it come from an industry expert in the form of a direct quote.

• Explain why the industry is in the situation or is riding a trend. Again, quotes from others are less intrusive than your own voice. In explaining the why, you probably want to get into what Robert Ruark once called the "nosepickers" of the subject, those hidden and not-so-nice reasons why a situation exists or why a trend may be negative instead of positive.

• Have your sources evaluate the implications of the situation or the trend, including the influence of the "nosepickers", then conclude the piece with a pithy quote from either a top expert or a man in the field who must deal with the fallout.

How to organize your research

The first job of any round-up or trend is to find the experts to interview. By expert, I don't at all mean the leaders in a particular industry. Remember the pyramid of information discussed earlier.

If you want to find out how the newest Komatsu crane operates, you'll want to go to the operators, then the designers. If you want to know how well it is selling nationally, you'll go to the Komatsu division marketing manager, then the regional sales representative, then to a sales manager or two at representative dealerships, and finally to the salesmen in the showroom.

Finding experts, I've discovered, is mostly a matter of common sense and access to a library with good directories and an up to date phone book. One of the advantages of writing for trade magazines is the difference in reception by the top level of experts in a given industry. Most have long ago realized that having their name appear in a trade magazine is among the best publicity they can have while having their name appear in, say, a local newspaper or generalized business magazine is seldom as effective for their business.

As you move down the pyramid, though, don't expect the people you contact to have the same level of comprehension about the differences between a trade magazine and, say, the *National Inquirer.*

Most interviewees on the higher levels of the information pyramid understand that trade magazine editorial, by its nature, is interested in looking out for the good of the industry, even when it is engaged in an investigative piece that may blow the whistle on dirty practices. *The National Inquirer*, and more and more often your local newspaper, are looking for controversy that will sell copies.

The most cost-effective way to interview is certainly by phone, but you will sometimes need to go in person. In some industries, I've discovered, almost no one will provide any information until they meet with you face to face. In other industries, especially those driven by high-technology, the interviewee enjoys the convenience of a phone interview almost as much as you do. And to add to this potential frustration, the need for personal contact varies from region to region as well. I've seldom interviewed anyone face to face in California, but about half of the interviews I do in Utah have this face-to-face requirement.

Remember, professional writers have their questions in hand, but are ready to explore new directions when the interviewee wants to move from the main topic. One of the nice things about writing trend or round up articles is that your experts answers are always interesting—whether they agree or disagree.

If they disagree, you have the makings of a highly interesting controversy, which makes for reader interest. If they don't disagree, then you have a consensus which also can be satisfying to your reader because they will feel a sense of satisfaction in having their own practice confirmed, or maybe satisfaction that they are going against the grain.

The most thorough procedure for keeping the question responses straight is to develop a grid for the questions. You can be as creative as you want to in creating your own form. What I generally do is to write the question on the right side of a sheet of paper, split the remainder into "pro" and "con" sections (or whatever is appropriately positive and negative) and then put the quotes for each underneath, something like this:

PRO	CON
Good design is good design whether it is in a contract with the owner or not.	It negates the architect's role of protecting the owner.
—Jon Contractor	—Paul Architect

With such a chart, it's easier to organize the internal arguments within your article. Don't cheat the reader. With any argument, you should keep apples with apples and oranges with oranges. Several structural tactics satisfy this goal. Just a refresher from Freshman English 101:

Parallel structure. In parallel structure, you corral ideas into groups, then keep the presentation consistent from paragraph to paragraph. For instance, you group pro ideas A1, B1, and C1 together.

When you talk about the con ideas, you follow the same order with A2, B2, and C2. As you demonstrate how these viewpoints are resolved, you again keep them in the same order for the reader with A3, B3, and C3. If you maintain this sense of order, the reader will be able to follow the argument more easily (and is more likely to read the article all the way through). If you break these logical patterns up, writing about A1, then B2, then C3 and back to A2, then C1, etc., you will either fail in your article or you will be asked to participate as counsel for one side or another in an impeachment trial.

Topical structure. This structure is similar to parallel structure, except you put all the As together, all the Bs together, and all the Cs together. If we were rewriting the previous structure's ideas, we would have a paragraph with pro A, con A, and resolution A, then follow it with pro B, con B, and resolution B, and so forth. You'll notice that this is a good organizational strategy for longer pieces where several ideas will be developed.

Cause-effect. Although the first two strategies give you a good basis for handling just about any round-up, trend or show article, you'll find that other organizational structures can work as well.

One of the best for a trend story is the cause and effect structure. Simply put, you outline the cause and then explain the effect. In life, the effect generally becomes the next "cause." You can also reverse this process effectively, beginning instead with the effect and working back to the cause.

Problem-solution. The problem-solution structure is a good structure for round-up stories. It's as simple as it sounds, and can incorporate within it variations on the first three strategies we've mentioned. The only caveat for multiple problems is to keep the solution in parallel or topical order. If you present problems A, B, and C, then present the solutions in the same order. You can also present them in a topical structure—start with problem A and give solution A, move to problem B and give solution B, etc.

These rhetorical strategies have developed from our sense of dialectic logic. That is, our journalistic desire to present both sides and let the reader come to their own conclusion. Don't deceive yourself, though. Most of us will come down on one side or the other of an issue, and often it will depend on whether you view the world as an absolutist or a relativist. Very often, the weight of argument is unbalanced. Put another way, there may be only pro A and pro B, but there is con A, con B, con C, con D, and maybe con E.

When you discover that situation, you organize your ar-

ticle "dialectically." It goes something like:
Pro A, a good reason for—Con A, a good reason against
Pro B, a good reason for—Con B, a good reason against
But

—Con C adds a reason against
—Con D adds another
—And Con E is the capper!

Just a quick caveat. Developing a structure for these stories is simple. Filling that structure with interesting quotations
and insights is often time consuming and requires some mental effort on your part. Remember this if you remember nothing else from this chapter: Substance beats structure every time.
Which brings us to the most important element of these stories.

Make an evaluation

Evaluation is truly the key to success in round-up, trend
and show stories. Consider a reader's motivation for turning
to such stories. Most often, the subject is one that they have
questions about.

Perhaps their job requires them to meet next week with
other members of the company to develop a marketing plan
for the next six months, the next year, the next five years. Perhaps their job is to make a key decision based on a marketing
report. Perhaps they are considering their own business start-
up. Perhaps they are contemplating entering a new market.
Perhaps they are charged with upgrading the current equipment being used by the company.

Most of the time, what readers look for in these stories
are adroit evaluations given from a base of insight by a group
of knowledgeable experts.

Your respondents should evaluate the trend or situation,
but you must take responsibility to interpret how seriously the
response should be taken by the reader. In a sense, the rhetorical structure you choose will do part of the job—whether you
want it to or not. Consider the basic tactical consideration for

any argument: What gets remembered most is what you start with, and what you finish with. In that sense, your evaluation of the evaluations will color how the readers perceives the information.

You will discover as you write these articles that the conclusion generally requires just that—a conclusion. Most round-up, trend, and show stories finish off with a sense of the implications for the future. The round-up consensus is summarized, perhaps, by one of the participants. The trend story may bluntly state what the trend is, or more likely, what the next trend may be based on the current situation. The show story will wrap up nicely with an evaluation of what the participants learned, or saw, or heard, and why next year's show may be even better.

Special notes about trade shows

Show stories have a couple of important structural possibilities. If you've gathered in the notion that show stories tend to be an amalgamation of round-up and trend stories, you are on the right track. What makes a show story different from a round-up story or a trend story, I think, is the emphasis on what was presented at the show, from the physical merchandise shown by exhibitors to the mental merchandise offered by seminars.

This show "merchandise" can be displayed for your reader by comparing apples to apples, or contrasting apples to oranges.

Comparisons come in at a variety of levels. You may need to compare the worth of one seminar to another. Very often, especially for trade shows, you may compare (or contrast) the inventiveness, usefulness, or marketability of new products being shown to that of current products.

A good show article must contain a sense of comparison—either implied or explicit—to provide a sense of completeness for the reader. After all, the essential point of any type of show, meeting, symposium, or convention is to assess a current situation and then point to a future direction. In short, to compare, and then, to contrast. How is the new A

135

Company ditchdigger compared to the old B Company ditchdigger. Are those computerized controls upping the bar for future ditchdigging equipment? Or is it so much more pricey than the old B Company equipment that the B Company product will survive in the long run?

There were five presenters at the "Cool Ways to Find a Vein to Start Intravenous Drips" during the nurses convention. What did they say, and will it have any impact on the way nurses find veins in the future? Did one predict that a robot will take over the job in ten years? Compare what each said, then evaluate (or better yet, have an expert show attendee evaluate) for the reader.

Remember this as well. Any time you have an assignment to cover a show, you have the opportunity for three stories, not one. Your first story, naturally, is the show story (or convention story, or symposium story, etc.). Your second opportunity is a separate round-up story (where you decide the question to be answered). Your third story is a trend story (where the attendees tell you what trend or trends to watch for). So attending these industry get-togethers garners you three story opportunities—and usually many more—for the price of one.

That's cost-effective research.

Chapter 9.

What else can you sell?

To make a living as a freelance writer, or to make a significant part-time income for that matter, means staying flexible in the type of assignments you take on. It seems no two writers ever follow exactly the same career path. We all tend to make our own way based not just on our likes and dislikes, but also to an extent on our location and our ability to make significant contact with other people.

As I noted earlier, the potential markets for freelance material in the trade magazine world are as extensive as in consumer magazines, but that doesn't necessarily mean you shouldn't be willing to look outside the trade market occasionally.

I believe, in fact, that while it is professionally and financially satisfying to become a specialist in one or two areas, it is healthy for a writer to seek different types of markets or writing assignments occasionally. Stale writing generally comes from developing a formula and then writing to that formula over and over until it is difficult to break out of the mold. By writing other kinds of materials, however, you can keep your mind and your pen flexible.

Even within the trade markets, you can find ways to vary your routine. The bulk of my bread-and-butter articles are on-the-scene stories. But I try to place at least three or four pieces per quarter outside of this realm.

Is news viable to sell?

One area where trade magazines can offer the freelancer a change of pace is with news or issue stories. Most news stories in the trades are develop by a magazine staffer through a lead from either a press release or a phone call. To be honest, many would reject a news story from an unknown freelancer. When an editor receives such a piece from an unknown writer, he or she must spend considerable time checking the facts and making sure that the account of the news item is accurate. In short, a news piece from an unknown writer takes so much of an editor's time that most find it easier to do it themselves or to assign it to in-house staff.

If you submit a news idea, however, most editors are honest enough to pay some sort of finders' fee. They just won't assign the story.

Once you've done a few articles for an editor, have established your professionalism, and have demonstrated your knowledge of an industry's issues and players, pitching a news story becomes a different matter altogether. Credibility is everything in pitching a news story, but once you've established it with an editor, news stories are often quicker sales than any other type of article.

Consider: you probably are not in a position to gauge the true importance of potential news unless you have an ear to the industry and have developed a good network of contacts. Remember that news for trade magazines means industry news. Your story must have an industry hook to be of use to a trade magazine audience. The larger your network of industry contacts and experts becomes, the more likely you are to hear news that would be of interest to the industry at large.

In the last chapter, we talked about round-up and trend articles. For the freelancer just beginning a relationship with a magazine editor, round-up stories will tend to focus around topics the editor wants explored but doesn't have the time or staff to pursue. As you develop your knowledge of the industry and justify the editor's faith in your ability, often you can develop your own round-up and trend stories.

There are always exceptions. If you are already a well-established member of an industry and just moonlight at trade journalism, you probably can identify issues more quickly than the newcomer to the field. But be careful, you may also have developed a set of visible biases from working within the industry.

Before you get too gung-ho on news stories, however, take a moment to consider how cost effective they really may be. When I first began freelancing, I approached a national trade magazine about filing news stories from my home area because I knew they had no correspondent in the region.

As it turned out, the pay was just $12 per column inch, and because I had read the magazine over the years, I knew eight column inches would be about the standard. At the same time, however, this magazine's sales department was paying $1 per word to write special "inserts" they could sell advertising around. It took about two seconds to figure out which would be more lucrative, though less prestigious, for a freelancer.

Profiles outside the editorial well

In trade magazines, you generally see two types of profile stories: personality profiles and company profiles. Although they share the name "profile," they are as different as night and day.

Personality profiles are often done as a regular feature story, with the same constraint of ethics to accurately report the best and the worst—with restraint. For a personality profile in a trade magazine, the emphasis is usually not on what the personality has done wrong—a trend in the consumer press—but what the personality has done right.

As feature stories, company profiles often follow the same

dictum. You don't necessarily dodge the company's past mistakes, but you do emphasize the positive accomplishments it has made.

More and more frequently, though, company profiles are becoming the dominion of the sales department, not the editorial, as trade magazines try to expand their revenues. It works something like this: The advertising representative pitches the idea of a "profile" to a prospective customer. The customer pays a set amount of money and provides a list of potential "supporters"—generally vendors the company buys from—who will buy an ad to "support" the company's profile.

The profile, known in the industry as an "advertorial," is used by the company in its marketing. Most companies find this is a very cost-effective way of producing a marketing piece outlining their capabilities without spending the small fortune it costs to produce an unsupported brochure. To have the piece appear in a national or local trade magazine also gives the piece an additional cache by borrowing a bit of the magazine's good reputation. Then the company can boast: "As seen in. . . ."

These "advertorial" pieces are a gray area for many writers. On the one hand, they generally pay better than a standard story with a strict editorial focus. On the other, if you have set a high standard for yourself in terms of authorial independence, they can be very problematic.

The plaguing question: Is it puffery? Is it drivel? Is it the type of piece I'll regret having written on my deathbed?

These are questions you must answer for yourself, but I'll give you an insight into my thoughts because I frequently enjoy doing these kinds of pieces although I have also been known to turn them down also. As a rule of thumb, I won't agree to do a company profile unless I have the sense that the company is not only ethical, but also a leader within its market. If I know a company is unethical, either in dealing with its vendors or dealing with it customers, I will pass on the assignment. (By the way, don't start counting up the dollars you may lose by taking this position—it will make you ill if your goal is to make big bucks.) In the final analysis, I ask myself if this is a company I would be proud to work for, and if I can answer yes to that question, I take the assignment.

When you do take on an advertorial project, though, you need to understand you are straddling the border between freelance journalist and freelance publicist. As a publicist, however, you can still make "the truth and the whole truth" the keystone of your writing. That's where I set my standard for doing company profiles: If I don't think I'll be able to follow that standard when writing about a company, I turn down the assignment.

On a practical level, however, company profiles greatly increase your networking opportunities. The vast majority of people in these companies are basically honest and hard-working—in short very much like you are, just in a different industry. In terms of learning about the issues in your industry, a company profile will often give you an opportunity to take a "short course" in what an industry wants, needs, and expects.

A quick aside. I'm nearly fifty and I listen to rap music, reggae, alternative, John Pizzarelli, Pietasters and Mozart. You'll seldom find me at home dressed in anything but jeans. Some days, if there are no personal trips I need to take, I may stay barefoot the entire day and forget to shave. In short, I can be as slovenly as anyone you've ever met. But . . . if I am interviewing a banker, I'll be in a starched white shirt with a crisp collar and a conservative gray suit. If I am interviewing an architect, I'll be in "uptown" casual clothes. If I am interviewing the president or officers of a large general contracting firm, I'll be in a tie. For a small firm, the tie usually goes, but otherwise I'll be in Dockers and a button-down casual shirt. If I am interviewing a field superintendent, I'll be in jeans, a work shirt, and work boots.

The reason is simple. Interviewees are often either nervous or judgmental, so if you match the way you dress for the interview to the way they dress for work, it paves the way for trust. For company profiles, trust is often more important to getting the job completed than your writing ability. Sad, but true.

By the end of a profile, however, provided you conduct yourself professionally—pay attention to detail, ask detailed questions, dress to a standard appropriate for the company's top management, make an effort to understand the company both in a logical sense but also with empathy for their concerns and needs—other writing opportunities may open up. Why? By acting like a professional during the course of preparing the profile, the company's management should have come to view you as what you are: a written communications expert.

The open door for experts

Every industry's needs are different, so this section will be filled with glittering generalities that may lose their shine in the bright sun of daily work. In construction, for instance, I've found almost no one who wants a manual written except the supplier companies. Because the majority of these manufacturers are located far away from my hometown, and because I get a bit grouchy when I travel much, I have not developed this particular skill within my main focus industry. In Chicago, the situation would be different.

Nonetheless, the opportunity comes by from time to time to do such a chore for a different type of industry. As a guideline for myself, if the work isn't too technical, I'll try my hand at it. On the whole, I've discovered I'm better at personnel manuals than computer procedures, so I avoid computer manuals. One of my mentors, Joe Evancho, Sr., has written a variety of manuals for the automotive industry which he specializes in. But then, he lives in Detroit, not Utah.

As you develop a name and an acknowledged expertise within an industry, you'll be approached more and more by individual businesses who want you to produce copy that they either don't know how to do or don't have time to do. Here's just a brief overview of these added opportunities for experts.

Editing new magazines. One of the first opportunities, naturally, is going to the other side of the desk as an editor, either replacing an existing editor in a magazine or as the editor of a start-up. Start-ups are becoming more commonplace than ever before in the trade magazine industry because not only is the nature of work changing, but also the nature of product and service distribution. The speed of change in an industry can be astounding, and the need for a magazine to adapt can make changes occur literally within weeks.

Patrick Clinton, in his *Guide to Writing for the Business Press*, cites the rapid change that went on in the hardware business. Within just about a two or three year span, the entire industry shifted from sales through thousands of small retail stores to sales through the "big box" home improvement warehouses such as HomeBase and Home Depot. These stores actually affected many elements of the residential construction industry because they captured—and have held—the do-it-yourself market and the small contractor market. Independent lumber stores have moved increasingly into sales to commercial, large residential construction, or supplying these warehouse stores, and have practically had to abandon the small customer.

Market changes shift the editorial emphasis in the relevant trade magazines dramatically, causing some to fold even as new ones began. As I write this chapter, I can name four national magazine chains that are planning to begin a regional edition for the Utah-Idaho market within the next 18 months. I know this because, as the expert in the region, I've been contacted by them.

Public relations opportunities. If straddling the border between journalist and publicist didn't bother you, you could find a variety of opportunities for writing copy on a freelance basis for companies that get to know you. As a lone freelancer, you generally can offer a better service for small companies than an ad agency or public relations firm.

Both types of agencies have a high overhead which figures into their price and makes them unaffordable for smaller companies. As an individual freelancer, you can charge a higher rate for public relations work than you may get for writing magazine articles and still come in at a lower cost. But you also have another tremendous advantage if you present yourself professionally. Agencies are members of the advertising industry. You, on the other hand, are a member of the same industry as the company you represent. That distinction is important, because the companies you work with should have more faith in your ability to understand their needs.

The variety of assignments from companies also help keep you from getting into a rut by just writing magazine articles. You may find you have an opportunity to produce newsletters, write news releases, write brochures, do the copywriting for ads or catalogs, develop technical or procedural manuals, or even help with annual reports for smaller firms that have stockholders. Another opportunity that is seldom mentioned is the possibility of either ghostwriting or collaborating on a book with someone from the industry.

It's not my intention to go into the ins and outs of these opportunities. Every industry's needs are different, so this section has been filled with potential work that may lose its shine in the bright sun of daily work. In construction, for instance, within my particular region of the country I've mentioned the lack of market for supplier manuals. There is a tremendous demand for software user manuals, but I so seldom deal with anyone but facility managers for the major software companies here that I have not developed the contacts to market this particular skill.

On the other hand, a colleague of mine in California has gone from nearly 100 percent freelancing for trade magazines to just about 100 percent writing instruction manuals for materials manufacturers and doing newsletters for associations.

On the whole, what you decide to do in public relations and other types of freelance copy aside from magazine articles will be dictated by the industries you decide to cover and the place where you live. My strong suggestion is that you keep an open mind about tackling such projects. When you get down to it, good writing skills can be adapted to almost any form. How pleasant it must be, for instance, for grant proposal readers to come across a new proposal that doesn't read like a legal brief. It would certainly make that proposal stand out.

If you want to supplement your trade magazine work with these kinds of assignments, I would recommend Robert W. Bly's *Secrets of a Freelance Writer* and *The Copywriter's Handbook* as a good overview first of how to get the business and consider pricing for it, and second, how to tackle a variety of public relations or advertising assignments. Another book to check on is Herman Holtz's *How to Start and Run a Writing & Editing Business* which can also stimulate your thoughts about other writing services for industry, government, and non-profit groups.

What about consumer magazines?

So many good books are available on writing for consumer magazines that I will limit what I have to say to some observations from my own experience. For those who want more about the ins and outs of writing for consumer magazines (including newspapers and the "general" business press), let me suggest Gordon Burgett's *Sell & Resell Your Magazine Articles* and *The Complete Book of Feature Writing* edited by Leonard Witt. A number of other good books exist, including some out of print books by Duane Newcomb which you might still find in the library, and you can always find new information in any new edition of Writer's Digest.

First and foremost, let me suggest that consumer magazines once paid much better than trade magazines. Nowadays the pay scale is about the same, but the consumer magazines are often deluged by queries and unsolicited manuscripts; the trade magazines seldom are.

Breaking into the consumer magazine market is seldom as easy or cost-effective as working with trade magazines, although I would acknowledge that understanding the consumer magazine's audience and their needs is often much easier. That said, consumer magazines which *mirror* the industry niche you work in can become a good source of additional income and, more important in many ways, increase your credibility as an industry expert.

Trying to get into a consumer magazine may also be good for you in the sense of expanding your outlook. In my case, the "shelter" magazines and in-flights which cover business and architecture are the closest mirror consumer magazines for the industry I cover. However, construction is actually three "industries," if you will, a commercial building industry, a residential building industry, and a non-building industry which includes everything from highway pavement to utility pipes to dams and harbor dredging—anything that starts with moving dirt.

For a variety of reasons, I prefer the building and non-building commercial construction industries although I have written successfully about residential construction as well. I do plan, however, to expand into the residential trades, and the shelter magazines, in the future, but I suspect they will never become a large part of my annual income.

Modern business gobbles up information the way the dinosaurs must have gobbled up swamp grass in the distant past. More and more writers who once concentrated solely on consumer magazines are learning the benefits, both monetary and intellectual, of writing for the trades. A well-rounded writer, though, who believes that writing is a craft, will try to perform equally well for trade magazines, consumer magazines, and non-magazine assignments. Anything less is self-defeating.

Chapter 10

How to balance workload, productivity, joy, and aggravation.

You will probably never get rid of all the stress inherent in meeting deadlines, but a professional writer learns to develop systems to help, instead of hinder, the work. In this chapter, we'll look at some of the systems I use myself. I have tried many—let me emphasize *many*—other systems, but have found these to be the simplest ways to reduce the irritation of the purely mechanical side of the business.

A quick confession. I am one of the top ten procrastinators in the world but have learned a very important lesson that frees up more time to procrastinate. The lesson? Do it now! Do it now! Do it now!

Yep, if you get the tedious tasks out of the way now, or as soon as they come up, this little procedural gimmick will soon give you more time to prune the roses, sun bathe on the patio, go to the basketball game, jet to the Continent or whatever your particular form of procrastination takes. Best of all, the guilt and angst you used to have about procrastinating will disappear. After all, you've already done it, so now you can wallow in the free time you've gained. No more looking for that lost phone number. No more digging through that pile of papers on your desk for the elusive fact you wrote down a week ago. File it now. Write it now. Put it away now. Cross reference it now. Done! Off to the Continent!

Help yourself by learning to file

Nothing smoothes the writing life more than learning to file, and nothing aggravates it more than failing to learn. I'm convinced of that. Until I developed a system of filing so that I could actually find what I was looking for, stories would take twice or three times longer to complete than they do now. Yet my filing system is not overly strenuous (if it was I wouldn't use it. No point in getting things done now so I can procrastinate if I'm wasting all that potential procrastination time looking for facts that I once held in my hand.)

Let me give my thanks to a little book called *File . . . Don't Pile! For People Who Write*™ by Pat Dorff, Edith Fine and Judith Josephson. This little book describes a complete system for getting control of the mess your files are in now, with excellent systems to track your marketing efforts, financial records, research and more. Although I don't follow all of their advice, I've incorporated some of their excellent ideas into my personal system with exceptional results.

Let's talk for a moment, though, about learning to file. There's no way around it: Filing is a tedious chore. But good files are a joy because you can retrieve material when you want it without spending an hour looking. In fact, that's the entire purpose of filing in the first place, isn't it?

The rule for your research files are very simple: When you plan to store research on broad topics—research that you easily believe will require more than about 20 individual categories, put them all together in one drawer and file each category alphabetically.

I do this for large main categories that I work with so a section of my files are just for commercial construction, a section just for publishing topics, a section just for residential construction, shelter, gardening, and related subjects, and a section just for writing and editing material.

Most of the material on organizing your office suggests buying colored files and using a color code to help you organize even further. Since I am something of a cheapskate when it comes to office supplies, I tend to use the plain old green hanging files and then put my manila folders within those files with no color coding. However, I make an effort to be sure the tab label is very readable.

In the first folder of each section, I keep a log of the files that are contained within the section with a page for each letter of the alphabet and have them numbered under the letter. For instance, on the first page of my log for commercial construction, I have folder A101 for Alder Construction, A 102 for Adams Mechanical Contractors, etc. I don't worry at all that Adams comes after Alder if you are alphabetizing because I can quickly look at the log's page for "A" to see where they are.

For files to be of any real use, though, you must come up with a simple way to cross-reference. One way to do it is to make cross-references in the section log so that under the A101 Alder Construction entry you might have several files, let's say C123, D111, and L102, listed as cross references. If you can maintain the diligence and discipline to keep this up every time you file something new away, it should work for you. I don't have this kind of discipline, however.

Instead I keep a separate file within each main section called X-REFS and a separate log in this file. In the construction section, for example, I will jot down the project on a sheet of paper clipped to the working file. As I go through the story or research process, I'll note on that paper what potential cross-reference files might be involved (more on working files in a moment).

On a typical construction project story, for instance, the architect and the general contractor are almost always interviewed, and sometimes a major subcontractor or owner. On this slip of paper I'll note: Riverton High School. Architect VCBO—V102. GC is Union Pointe—U101. Electrical contractor is Taylor Electric—T134. Owner is Jordan School District—

J112. When the story is complete, I'll pull this cross-reference slip and toss it into the X-REF file. Once a month I pull all the slips from the file and make the entries in the log. Normally all research material and the final draft of the story is filed in the general contractor's main file.

Taking care of this necessary chore once a month is easier for me than trying to do it on a daily, even hourly basis. There is some repetition, but actually very little time spent jotting the references on a piece of paper. I seldom spend more than 15 to 20 minutes a month catching up the X-REF file, but I am certain that I save hours searching for background materials using this method.

Single project files

When you are working on a single project that requires about 20 or less individual categories of material—a long feature article or perhaps a report or booklet—you can put these files together into what I call a single project file.

A single project file is just for that: a single project. But some projects are longer than others, so you may want to vary the way you set up your single-project file. Does it need its own section of the file drawer space? Could you three-hole punch material and collect it into a notebook? Would a single manila folder serve your purpose, or do you need an accordian file with many pockets?

For books, I generally begin by setting off a section of the file drawer. The nature of long projects almost forces you to expand the file space you need even as you make finer and finer divisions of research topics and materials. I start the filing process for a book by setting up five files for the project within a section of the file cabinet drawer. The first five files I label: Facts. References: Resources. Experts. Potential/related books or articles (called just "Potentials").

The idea for these divisions belongs to Gordon Burgett and can be found in a couple of his books. However, these divisions are only preliminary for me. Once I have a working outline, I expand the section to correspond to the chapters I've outlined with two other files. One I call "Additionals" for material to use in an appendix, bibliography, or index topics, and the other labeled "Potential Markets." That file contains both information on reaching target audiences, and ideas to expand into related projects. As I was researching this book, for example, I discovered that no good one-stop resource exists for those who want to write about the construction industry, so I'm considering putting one together.

Once the research material is compiled and I begin the actual writing, I file the rough draft in a three-ring binder. The reason, admittedly, is as much psychological as it is for ease of use. When you fill a binder, you can see that you are actually making progress toward your goal, and you can also begin to envision your work as a finished book.

For articles, I essentially use the same procedure, but on a smaller scale. For articles under about 5,000 words, I seldom go beyond a single file for the topic, but I do try to keep the facts, references, etc. in a separate area in the file and put a "potentials" sheet at the back. At this point in my career, most articles come as assignments, but when I am doing an article from scratch on my own nickel, I'll also file away potential markets in the back of the file.

Photos. Photos present a special problem. Since I take photos to send with articles, but don't by any means depend on my photography for a livelihood, my photo file is designed to match my article file. I print my own copyright notice on labels which I place on the back of prints. On the label is the copyright date, my name, my address, and space for a photo number.

The photo's number correlates directly with the main file where the article will end up. For the type of articles I do, as I have mentioned, most of my commercial construction file section is taken up with files for individual companies where I eventually end up putting article materials based on who the general contractor was (for construction) or what company the lead interviewee worked for. So if I have done a story on the new library addition at Brigham Young University and Jacobsen construction was the contractor, I'll number the photos consecutively: J101-1, J101-2, J101-3, etc. J101 is the Jacobsen file where the story research goes after completion. On the next Jacobsen project I write about, the numbers start where the first project's photos left off.

On slides, which I seldom shoot unless the magazine specifies them, I simply write the copyright date and my name on the slide and then the photo file number along the side of the sleeve. If it is a plastic sleeve, I'll cut off a small adhesive part of a Post-It{R} to stick on the sleeve so that I can write the information on. If nothing will stick to the sleeve, I'll say a few magic four-letter stress-relieving words and then put the slide into a page of clear slide-archiving plastic sleeves and stick the information to that sleeve knowing, even as I do, that if I send off the slide that way I'll probably never, ever see it again. For ease, I file the photos and slides in the file with the article they belong to.

Let me stress, however, that my photo filing system is based on the way I use the photos. I don't worry much about photo deterioration because, quite simply, the possibility that I will use the photos over a period of more than a few months is slim. Because I don't see much use for the photos over a long period of time, I'm not particularly picky about whether the paper they are filed in is acid free or that the adhesive on the labels might deteriorate the photo over a long period of time.

One reason photo filing and storage is somewhat difficult is because you must track not only the prints but also the negatives. Since I don't have a lot of reprints to do, I admit I'm fairly cavalier about maintaining the negatives file. Typically I just keep the negatives in the sleeve and envelope from the developing lab and label what story or project they go to on the outside.

If you are referring back to your negatives more often than I am, however, you may want to modify the numbering system I outlined above to reflect the negative's film number found along the sprocket line of the negative (i.e., J-101-1 would be renumber to match the negative number, becoming J-101-22, etc.)

There are a number of more complete and comprehensive systems outlined in books for freelance photographers, and if photography is going to be a substantive part of your business, I suggest that you check out the books listed in the bibliography. They suggest a more extensive but still "user-friendly" filing system and will give you information about how to maximize the preservation of your photos, slides and transparencies with the right archival materials.

Computer files. Computer files can be a bit more problematic. At first, I used the very simple Microsoft Works word processing program because it does just about everything I need to do, with very simple keyboard commands and mouse moves, without taking up much room like its bigger competitors.

I also used the inexpensive Microsoft Publisher to develop forms, rough out proposals, make up simple flyers, simple newsletters, and reports. While you can't lay out books or magazines very well with this simple programs, it is low cost and simple to use for about a million other things, and the Publisher 98 version will also help you design web pages.

Now that I've upgraded computers and work daily with the Microsoft Office programs, I still keep the same basic system for filing away stories, research, and financial information.

With the IBM platform, the ability to label individual files is limited to eight digits or letters, but with the newer Windows systems, , you can make a genuinely readable title for your file just like you can with MacIntosh.

With either platform, however, I've found that creating directories much like you would create filing sections is still the best method for work that will be ongoing. I have a directory, for example, that holds all the various templates, whether from Microsoft Works or Microsoft Publisher, for all of the forms I use. I keep a directory file for invoices, marketing, ideas, reports, books, Internet research, and general research. The general research directory is where I save information from Web searches until I can print out a clean copy(after removing the HTML codes). When I used a Mac, I had the same general files.

For articles, there are really two ways you can go. When I was on a Mac that had gigabytes of room, I made twelve directories corresponding to each month in the year. One file in each directory was a "to-do" list of what had to be completed for that month, regardless of what market it was going to. Naturally the other files in the month's directory were the stories I was working on and any computerized research information that would be used in them. This did and does generally take the form of interview transcripts. These monthly files were duplicated in the file cabinet as well, each holding the various project files for articles.

When I began freelancing full time, I was on an older PC and used individual 3.5-inch disks. Instead of the monthly order, however, I keep one disk per project. The reason is simple: many markets now prefer you send a disk with the hard copy of the article, or even send the disk and hard file after you e-mail a copy so basically, when I finish the story, the disk is ready.

To be on the safe side, however, I maintain a directory labeled "Complete" on my hard drive and just copy everything from a project disk to the hard drive before sending it off to the editor. An alternative, then, is to copy that material to a second floppy, or just leave it if you make a weekly back-up copy of your hard drive files. It's also a good idea to make a hard copy log of all of the article files in your hard drive so that you can find them easily.

A special note on the forms you create for yourself. Make a notebook and put a copy of the form in it with a notation on where to find the form on your hard drive. I put a copyright notice on the back of all the photographs that I send or take. The stickers are simple three-across mailing labels you can buy at any office supply store. One hard copy of the labels is in my forms notebook with a note across the top that the template is in c:\msworks\forms\piclabel.pub. Whenever I need new labels, it's a two-minute chore to find the template, load it, run the labels, file them, and get back to more important work.

The main key to filing is to have a system, and then work the system diligently so that you don't waste time or, more important, worry yourself sick by not being able to find the file you need.

Keeping track of projects and deadlines

The best guideline for keeping track of projects and deadlines is also to keep your system as simple as possible. While that's good advice, it's not always as easy to juggle deadlines for assignments and the information you need to track about queries or "spec" articles. Writing a book in addition to writing articles complicates the situation even more.

One of the biggest helps I find is to use a "project board." Different writers have different systems for these, but the main idea is to have a big board—preferably one you will look at several times during the day—with a list of projects and their deadlines. Some find that a calendar with the project listed in the deadline day works well for them. My experience is that most calendar boards have room for only the current month plus a few days.

Because I try diligently to schedule work ahead (I hate to feel I'm up against the wall for assignments), I just keep a running list of projects and their deadlines on a bulletin board directly in front of the table where I write. Use a black marker to keep up the list because it writes large enough to read without my glasses. As I write this chapter in early March, I already have a few assignments scattered through July, August, September, and November. Believe me, this is very positive psychologically as well as keeping you up to date on what you are doing. The plus is that when those invariable downtimes come on current projects, I can look at this board and maybe knock off an interview or do a little Internet search for a project down the road.

You will also need to maintain a log of the stories you are

working on. One way to log story assignments and other assignments is to create a form to keep in a notebook. *File Don't Pile* suggests different forms for different types of assignments, and that is probably the best system if you are diligent.

However, I've found that you must adjust to your personal circumstance. I keep my "log" on plain note paper in my Daytimer®. I boldly write the story's working title at the top, the slant of the story, and then the editor's name, phone number and the due date to the magazine under this information. After those entries I'll add the name and phone number of anyone to interview, and for each I leave room for their fax number and e-mail address. I do one page per story. Even if the basic research or interviews are going to be in several stories, I still copy that information on contact names and phone numbers in each story.

A log of stories with all the contact information in the Daytimer is important to me for two reasons. First, the Daytimer is always with me, so I always have access to the most important information I need right now, such as the phone number to call an interviewee if I am going to be late.

Second, as my wife pointed out one day, someone needs to know who and how to get hold of folks if something happens to you. Yes, it's a morbid thought, but if you get a bump on the head and are knocked out for a few days, then the people that are counting on you have to be told. Make sure you have more than a couple of people you can count on who know where you keep this information.

Perhaps I'm paranoid, but I have been on the other end as an editor and believe me, there is no worse feeling than calling a freelancer's house on deadline day only to find out they are in surgery and no one knows where there feature story is. I'm sure the freelancer was feeling worse, but I once had to put together a feature story in a matter of two hours. As it turned out, the freelancer had completed the story and it was on disk ready to send to me along with photos. Had someone known, I would have gotten the story and the freelancer would have gotten paid full price to help pay the medical bills.

Tickler files. Because the writing life is such a busy life, you need to be able to figure out what must be done on a given day: who needs to be called, what interviews must be done and so forth. You must also have a system to jog your memory when you are interested in doing a story, for instance, that may not really be a story for another year or so.

As I've mentioned, I keep a Daytimer and I use the daily calendar to schedule appointments and interviews, and to note deadlines. As a tickler file for the upcoming month or so, a Daytimer is a convenient tool. You can make your own, of course, using a notebook and a three-hole punch, but the small investment for the most basic of Dayrunner® or Daytimer® systems is very cost-effective compared to the time you spend doing your own.

Unfortunately, though, I haven't found any of these systems particularly effective for "tickling" the long-term information I need or for holding, say, large pieces of information such as clippings or project information that I may have gleaned from various sources. For that, I use a manual tickler file system that I learned courtesy of McGraw-Hill's Dodge Construction News division which must track construction projects, often through several years and phases of work. Dodge now uses a computer system to do this tracking, but their old manual system is still an effective, low-tech way to keep track of things.

First you get two sets of dividers. Perhaps you will want to buy a single desktop file to hold the materials, or you can keep them in an appropriate drawer file next to you. The idea is to have the first set of dividers set up for 30-day increments (two sets of 30-day increments). As you come up with information or material you want to refer back to in, say, two weeks, you file that information on that days date. Each morning you take out the information you have scheduled to use for the day and either use it or re-file it at a future date.

The second set of dividers have monthly headings. In here you put information that you won't be using in the next 60 days, but plan to use farther down the road. If you are going to need it more than a year from today (unlikely in most cases), you write the year you need it on the top of the page. At month end, you transfer the information from the upcoming month's file into the "days" file as appropriate. Simple, but effective.

Contact tracking programs. I have used the *ACT!* (Automated Contact Tracking) program for several years now, and I will give an unsolicited endorsement to it. One of the many features I like about it is that it can be modified in a variety of ways to suit your needs, such as pop-up menus you can modify so that you can keep track of what procedures you've completed for a client, such as "Mailed query", "Received assignment", "Faxed 1st draft", "E-mailed/Regular mail completed draft".

If you are very disciplined, you can keep all of your contact information, to-do list, tickler file, etc. on a contact tracking program. One major benefit of most tracking programs is the ability to generate labels so you can do mailings to your customers. Some, like ACT!, have built-in word processing so you can generate invoices and all correspondence in one convenient location. And one of the program's best feature is a "History" screen that shows you what actions and results you've had with the client or source before.

If you need to generate a database from ACT!, there is a method to transfer the information back and forth from a more general database program such as Microsoft Access if you need to expand the database functions. For example, I'm working on a resource guide for construction writers, so I am moving the basic contact information on construction trade magazines and associations from my ACT! database into Access to allow me a simpler method of formatting the information for publication.

You've probably noticed, however, that I use a paper system for keeping track of my everyday work. While I think contact tracking programs are wonderful, they do have some drawbacks. For one thing, you need to back up the database on a regular basis. That's easy enough when you have just a few contact names, but when your base reaches into the thousands, it becomes another time-consuming chore unless you can afford massive back-up storage systems such as CyQuest.

The other drawback, of course, is that it isn't always convenient to lug a computer around, even a laptop. You're going to jot down notes and names and addresses wherever you go, and you won't always have your computer there to help. The speed of your computer can become a consideration as well. As I struggled to maintain my databases on an old 486, the time to load a base with hundreds of names and then search within that base for the names I wanted took much more time than simply flicking through a rolodex or opening a file drawer next to the desk when I want to make my next call.

That said, a contact tracking program can help build your business in ways you don't always anticipate at first. As I said, I'm using the data in mine now to help build a useful, and hopefully profitable, resource guide for publication. I've used the program to build lists of people to market to, of course, but also lists for sending public relations material for my occasional clients. More often, I rent my list to clients. In terms of reconfiguring information to a one-time, customized need, a database is hard to beat.

Keeping track of what you owe and what's owed to you

I am not now, nor have I ever been, a trained accountant or bookkeeper. The information I am about to impart is based strictly on the practice that works for me. By all means, you should talk to an accountant before you set up your books! An accountant can help advise you both about the tax consequences of what you will be doing and about what kind of bookkeeping system might be right for you. What I'm about to tell you is rudimentary. For a more detailed discussion, you should get a copy of *Small-Time Operator* which is one of the best overviews of keeping accounting records for a small business.

Invoices. You want to get paid—that's the whole idea, isn't

it? Your invoice to publications you write for can be as simple or as complex as you want them to be, but generally you need to make sure at a minimum that the following information is on the invoice:

1. Your name, address, voice phone, and fax phone if you have one. An e-mail address is still optional in 1999 because most places won't send confidential financial information over the Internet unless it is secure or encrypted. You'll use email to correspond with editors, but not with the financial office.

2. Your Social Security number. This is a must. No one can pay you without it.

3. A brief description of the work you did. On my invoices that includes the story title; date of submission or publication; number of words, column inches or whatever measure; the rate of pay for that measure (i.e. 800 words at $.50 per word); the number of photos and the rate of pay (i.e. 5 photos at $20 per photo); and the total amount in a column to the right-hand side of the page. For multiple stories, you can stack these on top of each other, and then total up the totals column at the bottom.

4. (Optional) A listing of the rights you are granting to the publication. For instance: First North American rights for "Jurassic Park Theme Ride" and one-time rights for photos J104-01, J104-02, etc.

5. A job number or invoice number. This can be as simple or as complex as you want to make it. I generally just start with "01" at the first of the year and number as I turn in the next invoice, i.e. 9901, 9902, 9903. If you write a variety of different manuscripts or take on a wider variety of jobs than just magazines, you could use a five-digit number where the third digit is a code for the type of market. For example, 99101 would be the first magazine article of the year, 99201 would be the first

newspaper article, 99301 would be the first private business brochure, etc.

A necessary aside on copyrights.

About copyright. First of all, you own your own article and photos. A magazine is paying for the use of this property. The accepted standard on a never-before-published article is First North American rights, which means the magazine is paying to run the article first throughout Canada, the United States, and Mexico. You can, then, sell the same article to a magazine in South America, and sell the exact same article to magazines in Europe, Asia, and Australia.

You could even specify it even closer. Let's say you grant "First United States and Canadian rights." That would mean you could immediately publish the article in Mexico.

You could also modify the phrase to be "First North American English Language rights," and again, you could publish in Mexico by translating the article into Spanish. In fact, I have a colleague who speaks and writes fluently in Spanish, and he does just that.

Frankly, I seldom write this on my invoice. The exception is the first time I've written an article for a magazine and don't have "warm and fuzzy" feelings toward the people I've talked to there. In that case I usually specify the exact rights and then gauge what I'll do next time based on the way I'm treated and the speed of payment.

The Internet, however, has thrown a monkey wrench into the traditional rights system. Many magazines post the features from their paper issue into an online, electronic issue. Because it is a different medium, you should get paid again unless you specified that your article could be used there. But often no one tells you it is being used in that way, so unless you check the web site of the magazine, you won't even know.

And then the fun begins in terms of trying to collect. Although the courts have already ruled on this situation several times in the writer's favor, a favorite tactic is to take the matter to court because most writers don't have the time or won't waste the money to go to court for a $400 article. Fortunately, being an obstinate breed, enough have to set precedent. That's why you are now beginning to see consumer magazines and larger trade magazines sending contracts after the verbal assignment which, when read carefully, show you are signing away the Internet rights.

Don't just show me the money, show me where it goes

This is as simple as I can make a system for keeping track of the paperwork surrounding your business expenses and revenues, so here goes.

Accounts receivable. Set up a file in your cabinet labeled "Accounts Receivable." Into this file you put invoices that you've mailed off. When the check comes, there will usually be some sort of statement attached, usually as a tear off sheet that has your invoice number on it or a description of the article you wrote. Staple this to your invoice and move the invoice into your quarterly file, which I'll explain in a moment.

Accounts payable. If you have month-to-month expenses such as a loan or car insurance (assuming you only use your car for work-related trips), or advertising your services in a magazine, for instance, you can set up an accounts payable file with the billing information you need to stay on top of these monthly costs. Once the bill is paid, transfer the paperwork to the appropriate quarterly file.

Cash management. You will end up spending money every month on such things as film and photo development, luncheons, gas, paper, printer ink and other incidental expenses. You can develop a form to track these expenses—*File Don't Pile®* has a good one. Because my expenses related to trade writing tend to be very simple and repetitive, I mainly keep an envelope where I put the receipts after I've written the amount down in my ledger. Once the month is up, I put this receipt envelope in the appropriate quarterly file.

Quarterly files. Sad to say, you do need to pay taxes and FICA quarterly on the profits from your writing. Although I generate an income/expense statement from my accounting program, I may need to back up what I claim with proof, so I keep a file for each quarter of the year. Into that file go all my paid invoices for the quarter (income), all incidental cash receipts (expense) and a summary of ongoing expenses, such as loans or advertising, paid to during the quarter. That way, if I am ever audited, I have the "proof" of what I've done right there. At the end of the year, it all goes carefully sorted into a good manila envelope labeled "Income and Expenses, 19XX, or now 20XX."

Some additional things to note. First, bookkeeping is boring for most people, but if you pick one day each week to keep on top of it, it is less irritating that if you wait until the end of each month to figure your expenses and realize you misplaced the receipt from the camera store (if you paid by check, though, go ahead and write it down because you can prove the expense through the cancelled check).

Second, although I'm no accountant, I do know that the IRS still considers the home office deduction to be a red flag for potential audit. Within the next 20 years, as more and more people telecommute or open their own business when they are "downsized," I think the situation will change, but it hasn't yet. My accountant says the situation is about to improve, but we'll wait to see if any of my friends get audited.

Third, check with your accountant about the best way to go about your bookkeeping. I have been doing mine on an old version of the relatively simple Microsoft *Money* program which is similar to the home version of *Quicken*. I don't particular prefer one over the other, but the Money program came with the computer for free, so I've used it.

At the end of this year, though, I plan to go back to the good old fashioned double entry by hand. The only advantage I've seen in using the computer program is that it generates a number of reports for you. The disadvantage is that you must wait for it to come up, you must back it up every time you use it, and you must designate a category for every entry, so if something out of the ordinary gets paid for, you can sit there trying to think up a name for it, and the next time you enter something similar, you may come up with a different name.

That said, I will only be accounting for writing where I am working for someone else using the hand bookkeeping method. My publishing efforts will definitely be accounted for using a good computer accounting program.

Managing your daily work

By far, the most difficult thing about freelancing is managing time. Writing is the easy part. The tough part is finding time for all the attendant chores so that I can write.

In any given week, I'm generally working on four to six stories, three of which are usually due the following Monday, two of which are due in two weeks, and the last, fortunately, isn't due for a couple of months. I'll interview six to eight people during the week—hopefully by phone—transcribe the interview, jump on the Internet from one to two hours a day, try to carve out an hour or two per day for my own marketing efforts, including networking lunches often taking more than two hours because of the drive to and from, use an hour or two per day to go over research materials and outline questions for interviews, carve out another hour or two to work on this book, and then go to my son's football or hockey or baseball or lacrosse game. Did I mention keeping up the yard and automobiles and fixing the roof and the plumbing?

Frankly, if it could be that simple, the life would be easy. But about every other week, especially in the third or fourth week of the month, if you are lucky, you get a sudden rush assignment which must be done in two or three days, one that you can't foresee or build into your schedule.

I'm not going to introduce any earth-shattering principles for getting all of your work done. I will suggest you read any good book on time management. Even though it is an older work, Alan Lakein's book is still the best I've found on setting priorities and managing your work that way.

In fact, setting priorities is the only way you can get it all done. Lakein suggests labeling your tasks as A's, B's, C's and D's. A's are must-do today. B's are essentially should do today but can wait until tomorrow, C's are do today if you can get to them, and D's are things you can do in front of the television set or will go away if you forget about them.

When you write your "To Do" list—which you should do first thing every morning and do it religiously—your A list should be made up of those projects that will increase your long-term happiness. With such a criteria in mind, my teenage son's football game becomes an "A" for me, as does any activity which actively involves my children, grown or not. Know thyself, Socrates advised. I long ago decided my long-term happiness centers on my family, not on my career although the career is important too.

The point is: you must set your own priorities based on your own goals; no one can do it for you. And when two priorities butt heads, you must find a way to reconcile them. I have often found myself finishing a story on deadline late at night or very early in the morning because I took the heart of the day's time to go to a family activity. On the one hand, I won't let the family down, but on the other hand, I won't let my customer down either.

The tickler file discussed earlier and the project board are both the starting point to plan your day's activity. Both give you visual reminders of what must get done and when. One thing I've noticed is that the old advice about writing discipline is the truest advice: Set a daily writing goal and stick to it. And set a daily time to write, and stick to that as closely as possible. As I mentioned in the paragraph above, there are exceptions. Don't let them become the norm.

I write daily between 8 a.m. and 10 p.m. When I say daily,

165

I mean Monday through Sunday. One of the drawbacks of the writing life is that it is difficult to turn your mind off. Better to just get it out, drain those ideas, and move on with the rest of the day.

But I don't just write at those hours.

I write *whenever* I need to write. In the construction industry, contractors and architects tend to have company meetings between 8 and 9 a.m. Then they are reachable in the office between about 8:30 and 9:30 a.m. before they are off to another round of meetings, site visits, or luncheons. The next site visit is from 1:30 to 3 p.m., there is the driving around to consider, then back to the office at 4:30 or so before going home. To interview them, your window of opportunity is often 8:30 to 9:30 a.m., right in the middle of the best time to write.

I don't indulge in much touchy-feely theory about when and how and where to write. Even if productivity slips a bit during the afternoon, and even more at night, as long as the writing gets accomplished, taking more time to do it doesn't matter much. Some days the words flow so easily you are amazed anyone pays you to do this, and other days, the words come only after much difficulty and you think that there is no amount of money in the world worth the mental anguish you are going through. But the main point is you are being paid to perform a service, and the client, whether it's a magazine or a private company, is depending on you.

Everyone works differently. For instance, Ken Follett, I've read, does several synopses of his novels before he begins the first chapter. Tony Hillerman, on the other hand, figures out what information he wants to put in chapter one, writes the chapter, then figures out what he wants to put in chapter two. He may have a loose outline of the plot in his head, but he works it out chapter by chapter, not in advance.

I've found that I work both ways when it comes to writing trade stories. Some articles I will outline in advance; some I just work out the structure as I go. You must test the limits of what you can do from time to time, or you will never progress.

If you think you are a morning person, try writing in the afternoon or evening occasionally. You may find that, while it is not as good as what you produce in the morning, a thorough self-edit can get it up to the same level as your morning efforts.

I set goals within goals as well. Since book writing must be in addition to a daily career of writing magazine articles, I set a daily goal of 500 words just on a book topic. Because book writing and publishing is central to my long-range career goals, I faithfully do this daily at 8 a.m. while the contractors are in meetings. Most days, I double this goal, and occasionally quadruple it. That's the reason to try for a particular time period each day as well as being flexible about writing at other times during the day.

Take a day "off" each quarter. Maybe the most useful advice I can pass along is to take a "day off" once each quarter. Don't write that day. Don't interview. Don't file. Don't keep your books. Scrunch yourself up in your most comfortable reading chair, or lounge on your patio, or sail out in your boat—whatever relaxes you the most and requires only minimal physical exertion once you are in place. Take a pad with you though, because you *are* going to write something.

At the top of the pad, write down where you would like to be in one year, and what you would like to be doing. Under that, write down where you would like to be in five years, and what you would like to be doing.

Well, all of a sudden, you have adjusted your goal in life, haven't you. Now take stock. Write down the projects you have on hand right now. Are they the kind of projects that will take you where you want to be in a year? In five years? Probably some are, and probably some are not.

Next, let your mind brainstorm for a minute about projects you would like to write, whether they are trade magazine subjects or not. When I do this exercise, I usually come up with some trade subjects that I'd like to write about over the next few months, but I also tend to come up with book ideas or special reports as well. Very seldom do I come up with an idea for a consumer magazine article, or anything about computers, or anything about nutrition, or anything about travel.

Those subjects aren't a large part of me. I enjoy the construction industry. I love the publishing industry, and I enjoy performing arts. Most ideas I get fall into one of those three categories because, well, that's me. Your ideas will fall into your own categories because you are you.

Look at your new ideas. I'll bet they are connected in many ways with where you want to be in a year, and even in five years. Maybe your ideas for new writing projects don't fall within the scope of the markets you now write for. If not, it is time to start planning to go after new markets. Not all at once, maybe, but if you set aside a little time each day, an "A" time, to research and contact those markets, you'll have a much happier perspective on life.

Taking this day each quarter will reward you and enrich your life beyond your imagination. With a sense of perspective, you'll see that the writing projects you take on, often in unexpected ways, are helping push you to your goals. Actually, goals are just phantoms, mere idealizations of what you would like to be doing in a future moment. Real life is the journey you take to reach this fantasy, and the day off you take each quarter will help you appreciate the journey as much as the destination. Enjoy it.

Chapter 11

How to edit yourself before the editor does.

Start with good planning

Editing yourself is one of the most challenging aspects of writing whether you are writing for Construction Specifier or for Esquire. The reason is simple: Self-editing requires you to shift your mental gears, so to speak, turn the writing vehicle around, and head in the opposite direction.

In the previous chapter, I mentioned the necessity of setting aside a consistent time every day to do nothing but write. The same is true with editing, I've found. It is very helpful to set aside a specific time to self-edit, and my experience has been that it is better to schedule that time a few hours after your writing cycle. I'll ignore this rule occasionally, especially under deadline pressure, but putting some time between your daily writing stint and your editing cycle gives time for your interior critic to flex and stretch and get ready for a careful look at what you've done.

In my experience, when I begin to self-edit shortly after writing, I will re-word existing material even though it may already be fine, and I will often add material which later is cut

169

by the magazine's editor (and rightly so). The problem is that my thinking process is still in writing mode even though I'm supposedly editing.

I write in the morning. If I wait until later in the afternoon to edit, I come at the piece with a more critical eye and a pen that bleeds red ink all over the page, usually chopping unnecessary phrases and refining words rather than adding more explanation or superfluous material.

By now you've noticed that I am a big believer in procedures. Good procedures, I feel, are part of good craft. Consistent procedures, I believe, free your imagination because you can concentrate on the important part of the work, not on the details of how to go about the task.

For every writer, procedures develop with experience. I can only tell you what works best for me, and urge you to experiment with what works for you. For self-editing, I use four "sweeps" through an article to get a piece into shape to mail off. By sweeps, I don't mean a simple scan of the article, but a thorough reading.

Each sweep that I make, though, has specific goals. When I am doing sweep number one, I don't try to find the errors involved in sweep number three. On the other hand, if they leap out, then I circle them because if I don't, I'll spend my mental energy in the rest of the sweep trying to remember that one particular goof. And the reverse is true: if I spot something in sweep four that should have been caught in sweep 2, I'll stop to fix it and then continue the sweep. It's human nature to have a mind that wanders. The trick is to let your thought wander away, and then encourage your thought to wander back to the work at hand.

The first editorial sweep—completing the rough draft

To start the editorial process rolling, I generally go over familiar territory. Before writing an article, I have analyzed the magazine's needs—what belongs and what doesn't belong in an article on its pages. Most of the time I have gone through three or four articles noting what questions each paragraph answered and have then based a list of questions for my own article on this research.

Now I go through the current article first to make sure this list of questions has been answered. After all, if I didn't think the reader wanted the answer to the questions, I wouldn't have written the article in the first place.

One element I look for at this point is whether the interviewees are answering the questions through a direct quote or whether I am answering the question from an inference. While a balance should be struck between these two approaches, I believe most trade editors would rather have answers to key questions come from the mouth of an industry expert, not the writer, and I try to follow this dictum.

Sometimes a question has gone unanswered, so I make a note to follow up with the interviewee if I forgot to ask the question originally. If it is a question that was asked, but doesn't have a clear-cut answer, then I'll make note of that in the article.

Next check the article's thesis against your original thesis or slant. Are they still the same? Did the results of your research modify the thesis? More importantly, does the sum of your answered questions support the thesis sentence you have, or does it need to be modified to fit the facts?

The second sweep—a "baseline" edit

"Baseline" is word that means different things to different people. To me, a baseline edit is an attempt to make sure that all the necessary elements are in the piece, in an order that makes sense, with a "voice" or tone that's consistent, in a way that answers the readers' main questions.

Don't try a baseline edit before you have a completed rough draft. What happens most often is that your article takes on a life of its own, often running away from the points you were trying to make with all the enthusiasm of a wildfire. When you are going through this baseline edit, ask yourself the following questions:

1. Has an answer been provided for every relevant question? The point of any magazine article, you can argue, is to satisfy the reader's curiosity. In trade writing, the curiosity you most often ore satisfying is basically educational in nature: What process did this other company or individual use that I could profitably incorporate into the way I work, and what process is giving my competitor an edge?

2. Has every quotation's speaker been identified and given a job title or designation in the first reference to them? (i.e. Dave Layton, vice president of Engineering for Layton Construction). Although a baseline edit is primarily concerned with content rather than grammar, this particular mechanical element of identifying a speaker and a quotation has potentially serious legal consequences, so I include it as part of my first, second, third, and fourth sweep.

3. Identify potential problem areas in the article: Unclear language, such as quotes that have an abundance of pronouns and non-specific terms. Although probably clear in the context of the interview itself; generalized terms and pronouns seldom carry enough meaning to be interpreted accurately by the reader. This is another good reason to run quotations past the interviewee before you publish. Most of the time the right word jumps out at them when they realize how barren their quotation can become on a flat piece of paper.

Rough and abrupt transitions are another area to correct here. Sometimes the cure is simply a transition word or phrase, i.e. "for instance", "similarly", "moreover", "consequently", "frequently", "occasionally", "but", "however", "although", "though", "even if", etc.

As a rough rule of thumb: if a transition word won't fix the problem, you usually have either a lapse in the logic of the order you are using, or a problem in adding material that doesn't belong at all.

A lapse in logical order is usually simple to fix. If you are using space, for example, as the way you order material, you may have started describing things to the east, jumped across to the west, hopped up north, and stopped back in the east before you headed south. If you are using one of the argumentative orders, you may have thrown three unrelated "cons", A, B, and C, up against a single "pro", A, before going to pros B and C.

If you added material that doesn't belong, it simply may go elsewhere in the story. If it doesn't belong in the story at all, you may have a potential sidebar. I recently completed a story on the electronics of a county-wide traffic control room. I had material on the fiber-optic cabling that went to the traffic signals, but it didn't fit, so I developed a sidebar that gave a concise explanation of all of the systems the control room monitored.

Other potential problems to be corrected here include tables, sidebar materials or charts that must be formatted.

4. Make sure the lead organizes the story, and more to the point, the story substantiates the lead. If you were concentrating mainly on writing the body of the article, you sometimes go back to your lead only to discover that it isn't what you've written about at all.

When this happens, you have some options other than completely rewriting the story. For a variety of good reasons, editors in consumer magazines often insist on receiving exactly what they were promised, which usually includes the precise slant decided on. In trade magazines, though, I believe most editors are willing to grant some room and are not as dependent on the precise slant as long as the story is still pertinent to the issue they are planning to produce.

If you are writing about a library, say, that was supposedly built under a design/build contract and you have written in the story that it is actually a construction management contract with the architect hired separately, you may still be okay if the magazine is doing an issue on library construction. If the topic is design/build, you must do another story. However, it might be possible to get the editor to run the story in a later issue about construction management.

Theoretically, you should have noticed the discrepancy early in the research process. But editors can sometimes be a vague as writers, unfortunately, and this editor might not have made it clear how or why the story was going to be used.

Even if you must stay on the agreed to topic, all is not necessarily lost. Trade writing—all writing for that matter—is made up of choices. You choose to emphasize this, de-emphasize that. Often the addition of a few sentences or the extraction of a few can turn the piece in the direction you want.

If it won't, however, you are left with only one other choice: Write a new article or admit to the editor that you can't provide the article promised.

5. Make sure the conclusion substantiates the story and the lead. In nearly half of the trade stories I do, I break this rule. And I do so with a light heart and clear conscience.

That said, writing a conclusion that summarizes what you have told the reader and what consequence that has for the reader is a tried and true method of ending a story. Deviating from such a conclusion requires some thought.

Many trade stories, unless they are very long features, don't allow much luxury to round up the article's theme. On shorter features, say 1,000 to 1,400 words, I often use two other concluding tactics. The first is what you might call the "For More Information" tactic where I tell the reader how to find out more about the topic. The second is the "Summary Quote" which is simply a quote from one of the folks mentioned in the article which reduces the point of the article into a pithy suggestion for future action. While this method is similar to the summary conclusion mentioned above, it's very abruptness gives it more impact. Even better, it's a teaser for skimmers to go back and read the entire article.

6. Ending the sweep. Is your information correct? Does it answer the relevant questions raised by your thesis sentence? Does that thesis get proven or illustrated by the contents in the

body of the article? Is the reader left with the feeling they have learned something? If all the answers are yes, it's time to make the next sweep.

The long third sweep—find the peccadillos

All magazines operate under a basic set of style guidelines. For most, the majority of guidelines are either from the Chicago Manual of Style or the AP Stylebook for punctuation, spelling, restrictive clauses, reference form, etc. Also, magazines develop their own customized style guides over time which allow them to integrate an industry's jargon and usage into the basic Chicago or AP form. The larger the magazine, the more likely this guide is codified in a written manual. Smaller magazines, though, often have the style guide in their editor's head, not on a sheet of paper, which means you must study a few issues to get a sense of it.

A good example of these unwritten guides sometimes comes with the word "said" in an attribution. AP practitioners almost always prefer "said" as the lead in to a quote attribution:

"It was necessary to destroy the village in order to save it," said the Armed Forces adjutant.

Some magazines, however, prefer the present tense to give more immediacy to the quotation:

"It was necessary to destroy the village in order to save it," says the Armed Forces adjutant.

I think you can see the difference that one small word has in giving the reader either distance or immediacy. The point is not to argue the rightness or wrongness of the word choice, but to understand that style differences can be subtle to you, but jarring to an editor. If you have used "said" in every article run in the last ten years, then the article submitted using "says" is going to cause some minor irritation even though easily fixed with the Find/Replace toggle.

More important, the editor is going to wonder why you didn't catch it and make the change. A small difference, but it knocks a chink in your professionalism.

So the third sweep is concerned with just that: making sure your article shows you have a professional's grasp of the grammar, syntax, and punctuation required. If the magazine has a printed style guide of its own, ask for a copy. And don't assume a magazine which is part of a conglomerate of magazines is necessarily consistent with the rest of the company. McGraw-Hill, for instance, publishes its basic style guide, and the magazines it owns consistently ignore it in favor of their own, generally based on the AP rather than the McGraw-Hill guide.

There isn't enough room in this book to go into all the variations that may occur. Chances are that you developed your writing skills through courses in either journalism or English. If you were in journalism, you were probably taught under the AP style. If you were in English, you were guided by the Modern Language Association's style guide which is very close to the Chicago style.

One caveat: Most of the secretarial or business style guides are less than helpful in writing articles and even can be dead against common standards shared by the AP and Chicago guides. Don't use an office style guide for anything but writing letters.

A simple test can give you an idea of which base guide the magazine is using. Look for a sentence with a serial list such as "apples, pears, and peaches." See that comma before the concluding conjunction? That's 5.57 from the *Chicago Manual of Style*. No comma (i.e., ". . . apples, pears and peaches") is from the AP Stylebook. The good news is that many of the style rules within the two guides are similar. The bad news is that some are not.

Additionally, many magazines make up their own rules on titles and other style matters. For eight years I worked on three magazines where the only capitalization in the story titles was the first word or a proper name. With a change in administrations, I was back to the AP capitalization guide.

Trade magazines have a further issue that's important. With its combination of associations and technical terms, any industry's acronyms can be confusing. Both Chicago and AP call for spelling out the name of an organization in the first citation and then allow the acronym for the rest of the piece. But what about technical terms? Have you seen any articles at all in the last ten years which spell out Computer Disk Read Only Memory (CD-ROM)?

This is where the magazine's own style guide can be most useful. Sometimes it depends on the audience. If I am writing for Electrical Contractor, I'll never spell out UPS, which is an Uninterrupted Power Source, and I have no doubt readers will understand I am not referring to the package delivery company.

If I am writing for *Audio/Video Interiors*, however, I would definitely write it out on the first use because many homeowners and residential contractors who are not used to the terminology are readers in addition to engineers and electricians who would understand.

The same guidelines apply to industry jargon. While purists may argue that jargon should simply not be used (a fact drummed into the author from English 101 through English 610), trade magazines must typically compress a tremendous amount of information into a small amount of space. At the simplest level, there are the "replacement" nouns—sometimes acronyms, sometimes not—such as the names of organizations, product, equipment and materials, etc. And they can vary depending on the audience. Put "AAP" in Publisher's Weekly and almost every reader will read "American Association of Publishers." Use it in Modern Healthcare and it's the American Association of Pediatricians.

Another form of jargon is technical measures, categories, and specifications. I'm planning to build a new computer with an 8.4GB HD, ASUS 40X CD-ROM drive, EPoX MVP3G motherboard with 1MB Cache, 64MB of RAM using two 32MB

168-pin SDRAMs, etc. Computer builders and well-schooled users will understand what that means, most people won't although I think in twenty years, most people will.

Technical jargon is a shorthand way of saying what you need to say. Your choice is to write "advanced traffic management system" every time you refer to it, or to write ATMS which will give the intended reader the same basic mental picture you have.

As a writer, your first and foremost duty is to convey information. An ongoing problem is to know when too much is too much. While business and technical people can certainly comprehend the technical shorthand, it is still your job to be sure it is presented as a readable, interesting, informative article. Think of it this way: You can read, say, your computer's technical specifications in its handbook, and they are no doubt informative, but are they presented in an interesting enough way to remember them in a week? That's the challenge.

A related challenge creeps into this sweep. Make sure your acronyms are correct, and double-check to be sure you are using any technical terms correctly. If you refer to an audio mux, for example, audio/visual engineers and contractors are going to scratch their heads because a "mux" is a piece of equipment that transforms fiber-optic light signals into composite video signals.

While you are sweeping to make sure your language is clear, take a moment to review unspecific quotes or unclear quotes. This is a good time to call your source, read the quote, explain how it will not be as clear as needed on paper, and give them a chance to improve it in their own words.

Although this technique generally clears up the clarity problems, it is often up to you to decide whether you 1) quote "as is" with no modification, or 2) make some modifications based on the rules of grammar, not the sense of the quotation.

Before you decide on choice number 1, think about the potential consequences. The ability to express oneself is a learned skill, not an instinct, so some of us are better at it than others. Writers are often more comfortable expressing their thoughts in writing, but not orally. Remember: Most folks aren't writers, and, consequently, are often more likely to feel comfortable talking, but not when they write. While their grammar may not be precise, they often rely on writers to "fix" the grammar problems.

Should you? The answer is: Decide every case on its own merits. I once had a hard and fast rule never to change a quote unless the speaker had an opportunity to make it more sensible. (Note: I won't pull a quote unless the speaker is my client. If I am writing for a magazine, I let the editor know the situation and abide by his or her decision.) What changed my mind was a story that I wrote early in my career. I was unable to reach the president of a major local construction company so he could review his quote. His marketing manager read it over, thought it was great and said he was sure the president would be fine with it.

This president hasn't spoken to me since. In fact, he's labelled me a "yellow journalist."

As far as I can figure out, he's mad that I quoted him exactly, vernacular and all. He felt ridiculous. He can't swear he didn't say it, though, because I have it on tape. Still, the company threatened to pull their advertising, but eventually accepted an apology from the publication's sales representative.

Now I take it upon myself to at least clean up the grammar in a quote. And if I can't get hold of the speaker, I will put my best understanding of the referent word in brackets, and I will use ellipses liberally when they have rambled on. I prefer not to use ellipses, however, because when I read, I always suspect their use means the juiciest part has been left out.

The last item on this sweep is to smooth out the transitions between paragraphs, and between thoughts within the paragraph. Don't be afraid to use transitional "tags". They are the subtle mark of the professional writer, as long as you keep them subtle. Tags such as "For example", "likewise", "finally", "frequently", "unless", "when", "or course", "however", and their numerous cousins help move the reader from point A to

179

point B in a steady, logical progression.

Relative pronouns—"these", "those", "it", "they", "who"—and adjectival pronouns such as "many", "most", and "several", can also help tie ideas and points together, but should be used sparingly and when there is no mistaking the reference.

Don't forget specifics. A transitional tag "helps the reader around the turns, but specific details give them solid footing," as Sheridan Baker points out in The Complete Stylist. In this sweep, help your poor sentences bloom into flowers of lucidity by doing four simple things:

1. Change every passive voice sentence that you can into a active sentence with an active, descriptive verb. Sometimes, you can't. Passive voice, for instance, allows you to put the hero of the sentence where he can be more easily modified: Senator Foghorn, who himself has been shown to be a raging philanderer and mean to small children, called for the President's resignation. The appositive phrase in this example takes the spotlight from the basic information. "The President's resignation was called for by Senator Foghorn who has himself been proven to be a philanderer and mean to little children" gives you the information in an order that prioritizes the emphasis for that particular sentence.

2. Rework every "of", "which", and "that" you possibly can. A passive sentence often breaks out in these, but even an active sentence can suffer from this pox. "Which" and "that" can usually be amputated with little loss of fluid. Participles can modify antecedents directly: Change ". . . the truck which was heading south" to ". . . the truck heading south." So can adjectives: " . . . a project delivery method that was popular at the turn of the century" to "a project delivery method popular at the turn of the century." See? Even two words gone freshens the sentence. If you must use, choose "that." "Which," technically, should signal a nonrestrictive clause, but a nonrestrictive clause is basically an afterthought and not an integral part of

the meaning.

Verbs or verbals, such as participles and gerunds, can help cure of-itis. "Programming is the art of the utilization of numerical sequences of electrical pulses to create a matrix of information that can be translated into useful knowledge." How about "Programming creates information from electrical pulses in numerical sequences" instead?

Note that use and use of and their ugly sisters utilization of and utilize always lengthen your sentence but seldom add any real meaning. You should generally alter the sentence or cut them out altogether:

He uses an example to show . . . [His example shows. . . or He shows . . .]

Through [the utilization of an example] . . .

Her [use of] feasibility programming is effective.

3. Break up every noun "cluster" you can. As our society and business culture become more and more dependent on technology, we respond more and more frequently with a form of "technospeak" that encourages nouns in clusters. It's difficult to write about an industry without including some of these clusters which have become a lingua franca for new ideas and concepts which have no corresponding singular noun or no corresponding acronym.

In commercial construction, for example, "design/build" has developed a common currency to describe a method of delivering projects with a guaranteed price to an owner. I started to finish the preceding sentence with "to describe a particular project delivery system. Those three words constitute a noun cluster. They are perfectly acceptable—I would even call them the norm—in everyday conversation within the construction industry. If I slip this cluster into an article, few editors would question its use. Whenever I can break up these conglomerates, however, it makes me feel I've made a small but vital contribution to understanding and rationality.

4. Write without fear. Yes, your interviewee may have pro-

prietary information that shouldn't be shared. Yes, your inter-viewee and your editor may be afraid of hurting someone's (read "advertiser's") feelings. Yes, many folks you interview will fear that whatever they say will be held against them in a court of law (seriously, they do). And yes, you may even fear that by writing without fear, you will be too flamboyant and your words will be taken too seriously.

I like the way Sheridan Baker has phrased it in *The Complete Stylist*:

"We have become a nation of hairsplitters, afraid of say-ing Czechoslovakia's Russian tanks for fear that the reader will think they really belong to Russia,. So the reporter writes Rus-sian-type tanks, making an unnecessary distinction, and clut-tering the page with one more type-type expression. We have forgotten that making the individual stand for the type is the simplest and oldest of metaphors: 'Give us this day our daily bread.' A twentieth-century man might have written 'bread-type food.'"

If you fear misunderstanding because you write boldly and with a flair, don't be a writer.

A last quick sweep
This is your last chance to trim off the fat, but be careful. You may need to keep "that" now because it makes the meaning clear. You may decide to cut.

You walk a fine line here. You want your prose to be clear, but you also want it to have a voice, to "sing" as Nuwer says. To make it sing, shorter isn't always better (although it is about 80 percent of the time).

Watch out for the foolish hobgoblins of consistency that may rob your voice of its timbre. Although we need to follow the rules of grammar and punctuation, remember that meaning in English can expand through fresh syntax and context to high-light or emphasis.

For that same reason, though, words can often take on an

unintended meaning. In this last sweep, you must try to spot any quirks even though it will be difficult to read with fresh eyes.

It's also one last chance to consult your style guide for consistency in the nuts and bolts of your presentation. Magazines, unfortunately, always have their own quirks. As a general rule, most follow the Chicago Manual of Style, but a great many adhere to the AP Style, especially when their editorial leader comes from a newspaper background. Some are a hybrid of the two. Some use another stylebook such as the APA (American Psychology Association), and some are just simply on their own wavelength.

If you do a lot of public relations work—writing press releases and such like—and write for newsier magazines, it is probably better to learn the AP and just stick with it. Your magazine's copy editor can put it into the Chicago format. If you tend to work with book publishers or do academic writing as well as trade magazines, then Chicago is probably your best bet.

For heaven's sake, run spell check. It won't fix everything (oar will it?) As a former editor, I can tell you from long experience that the most knee-jerk negative reactions come from misspelled words. Most editors would even prefer the wrong word (except perhaps, there for their) correctly spelled. Misspellings, though, completely ruin your credibility as a professional.

If you have time, and you probably won't, have someone read the article aloud to you, or read it aloud into a tape recorder and then listen to it. Trust your instinct on whether the piece works.

Even with good planning, some pieces need more work than others. You actually learn more, though, from articles that don't go well. And usually the lessons you learn have less to do with your writing per se than your planning or interview techniques. What I've learned over the years I'll say quickly: If your writing doesn't sing, at least make it conversational, and watch out for the piece that writes too easily—that's where misinterpreted definitions and misinterpreted quotations fall most often.

Chapter 12

How to re-market your research

Research once, write often

The rewards of writing are many, but the tribulations are many more. Look at the practical aspect of being a writer from a factory manager's point of view. You have several elements that go into the "production costs" of article. You might call this, in accountant's parlance, the "cost of goods sold." Here are just a few.

First, we can identify immediate out of pocket expenses easily. There is the cost for mileage and parking, for phone calls, for paper to type up your article, and for the envelope and stamp to mail out the article. Your costs may include time spent photographing a project or a person, getting the photos developed, the extra postage to mail the photos, and so forth. Don't forget there's an expense to send the original query or to query by phone. You can identify all of these as project-specific expenses.

Less project specific, but still identifiable "hard" costs, are the overhead costs of doing business: the monthly phone bill, monthly rate paid to your Internet Service Provider so that you can have e-mail and the Web, the cost of the furniture and equipment you use, the cost of your office, at home or in a separate business location—hard costs include any expense where the provider of a service or supply item expects a check from you whether you sell your writing or not.

Less apparent in your cost scheme, however, is how much you actually pay yourself, and how much extra you spend doing too many of your own chores when you could spend the time more profitably. Many writers write for much less than the minimum wage. It's not fair, but it is the way the world is. The trouble is, many writers don't understand their costs, so they don't understand how little they are actually making.

Second are other costs that don't bear directly on your writing business as far as the IRS's Schedule C, but do bear directly on your peace of mind and the feeling that you are winning and not losing the writing game. If you have ever been self-employed, for instance, you are already aware that such elements as quarterly taxes and health insurance must be figured into any equation where the final amount is enough to pay the mortgage and buy groceries.

In fact, it is bearing the cost of health insurance and taxes that make writing magazine articles such a difficult business to do full time. In my humble opinion, article writers find themselves in a perverse situation. On the one hand, if you moonlight at writing while you have a full-time job, you can make much more per hour than you would at, say, 7-Eleven or almost any other part-time pursuit. On the other hand, writing articles full-time can drain your mental energy and economic security like no other pursuit I can imagine short of trapping a protected species for clandestine scientific research. A full-time writer must generate cash flow—and generate enough to pay the federal government, the state government, the municipal government, the insurance man, the utility guy, the electrical company, the phone company, the mechanic, the mortgage lender or the landlord, the grocer . . . the list of entities who want a check sometimes seems endless.

Where most writers fail financially, though, is not by spending their revenue on unnecessary things like food, but by squandering the potential of research.

The main expense of research is a soft cost: your time. Let's say you are well organized so you can research and write a 1,000 word article in 10 hours. It's not impossible because I have done it for almost ten years. If you sell that article for thirty cents a word, you will be paid $300.00. For illustration purposes, let's leave photography out of the equation for now.

On the surface, this seems like a fair deal: You make $30 per hour for ten hours of work.

But let's say you spent, oh, two hours finding the right magazine to sell to. And let's say you spent another four hours analyzing the articles in the magazine. All of a sudden, you're into this article for sixteen hours, and you are making $18.75 per hour. Still not so bad.

But wait, we've forgotten to take out some hard costs. Let's see. We need to pay taxes, federal, state, local, and FICA since we're considered self-employed for the purposes of writing this article. My accountant tells me that takes about 24% of my gross revenue, so that's about $228 left from that $300 sale. Now I'm making $14.25 per hour (at a total of 16 hours, not 10). Still acceptable compared to filling the Slurpy bin.

But there were other hard costs. I spent $5 on long distance. Three dollars for copies. Eight dollars for postage (Priority Mail + stamps for queries) plus an hour on the Internet I forgot about. I'm using several piece of equipment I've had to pay for, such as a fax machine, computer, hands-free phone, tape recorder, blank tapes, etc. Difficult to figure, but I sell about 10 to 12 articles per month, and I know a month's overhead expense totals about $150, so I'll chalk up $15 in extra hard costs to my article. Now my net revenue is just $197 after 17 hours of work. Still not so bad at $11.59 per hour.

Wait though, I had some more "unproductive" time this month. Let's see, I spent some time reading about potential markets for future articles. I spent some time reading books on how to write better. I spent some time at writers' meetings. I spent some time at industry meetings networking with folks to get story ideas. Let's say I sold 10 articles this month. Each article took 10 hours to research and write, but another two hours to "market" correctly. So that's 120 hours out of a 120 hour month, but I also plugged in the study and luncheons for another 60 hours, so each article cost me about 18 hours! So assigning that overhead to my $300 article which really netted just $197, I made about $11.16 an hour.

Still better than 7-Eleven—unless they pay medical and pension!

Give yourself a raise?

You are employing yourself, so you must do the same thing any employer would do: figure out how to get more money out of your production time without raising your production expenses by that same amount.

One thing you could do, of course, is figure out how to do the ten-hour story in nine hours—or as we've pointed out, how to do that sixteen hour story in about fourteen hours. You can make such an adjustment, and experience will teach you how. There are certainly 1,000 word stories I've completed in less than three hours. On the whole, long stories that took 16 hours to complete a decade ago now can be done in about ten or eleven total hours which is no mean feat. How? Now I know who to call first for both an assignment and for the right interview—and they know me well enough to take my call. I don't write any faster, I just research faster.

Three other methods, however, will help you boost your pay, not to mention your self-esteem, much quicker.

Sell your "research time" more than once.

This notion is not new to me and I give full credit to Gordon Burgett. I first saw this idea in *How to Sell 75% of Your Freelance Writing* and then in more depth in *Sell and Resell Your Magazine Articles*. The concept is disarmingly simple. You research a topic and then:

1. Sell many different articles—with different slants—to different magazines or newspapers; or
2. You sell the same article as a "reprint" to several different publications.

Let's look at these two methods one at a time.

Selling many different articles from the same research is effective, and has the added advantage of . I've used this technique again and again with good success. To make it work, you first "topic spoke", as Gordon calls it, by brainstorming different slants an article could take¾each slant targeted for a specific market.

If you research the construction of a jail, for example, one slant could be a case history of the jail's fabrication for a construction trade magazine. Another slant would be how to get the most out of your construction dollar for a trade magazine targeting jail administrators. A third article could be how to design a jail to be built inexpensively for a trade magazine that architects or designers read.

You can do articles on specific aspects of the jail's construction. If there is an innovative plumbing system, for instance, you can target a magazines for plumbers or for mechanical engineers (two different articles). You could talk about an energy saving lighting system in a periodical for electrical contractors, one for lighting engineers, one for public administrators, one for energy conservationists (four articles).

You could talk about the uniqueness of the precast modular cells in a magazine for pre-cast concrete contractors and installers, and the use of the crane to install these heavy modules in a magazine for crane operators or even equipment rental magazines (two more). The newer the jail, the more sophisticated the control of cells become, so that may be an article for a specialized journal. Opto-electronics are involved in many new security systems, so you may have grist for a magazine dealing with opto-electronic products or design (let's call this one more).

With a long-term process such as the construction of a large jail, you may even be able to do more than one article on the process of the construction itself by writing an update midway through the process and then at the project's completion (two articles). Once the jail is complete, there is usually a period of time when the new staff trains in the facility and goes through situational dry runs before prisoners are actually transferred in. This training period offers a follow-up on how the staff believes the jail will perform. And you follow-up again a year after the inmates move in to see if the facility has performed to standards (two more articles).

Now you have fourteen potential articles, eight of which you will be able to research all at the same time, and six which will require just a couple of hours of additional research at various stages. To put it bluntly, if you could sell all fourteen for $300 apiece, you would probably rake in a gross of $4200 for around 80 hours total work. If only life were that easy!

Let's say, though, you can query twenty-eight magazines (two for each slant), spending about thirty minutes each on a query. That totals 14 hours. Four of the magazines buy. It takes you an average of two hours to actually write and edit each story for a total of 8 hours. Since the articles are so closely related, you make only two visits to the actual site, taking up a total of 4 hours. Ten more hours are spent in 1) interviewing five participants and a consultant expert in jail security design, 2) transcribing interviews, and 3) reading a couple of articles about correctional design theory. Your absolute total for the four articles is 36 hours—and this is an absolute total because I've factored in the non-productive time as well in my estimate—so you are making more than $30 per hour, and clearing close to $20.

That's a theoretical total. I performed this very feat in much less time because I spent just 15 minutes on each query (knowing who to call) which cut the 14 hours there to 3 1/2 hours. Twelve hours were spent in interviews, but the articles took a total of only nine hours, so there's $1200 for about 27 hours worth of work.

You also will find a cumulative effect. Taking some time initially to analyze a magazine and then prepare excellent queries eventually gives way to being experienced enough with the magazine and the editor so that queries are a quick phone call.

No hard and fast rule exists for how much time and effort

you should spend to analyze a magazine. I think Burgett's approach, outlined in *How to Sell 75% of Your Freelance Writing*, has merit, but I have seen others. It simply takes as much time as it takes for you, and there's no way to compare the amount of time you need with the amount of time someone else would need.

What I will suggest, however, is to spend analysis time primarily on those magazines which cover your main specialty. You probably don't want your articles to be just "one-shot" articles in those books, but rather a foot in the door for future assignments as well.

In magazines outside your main specialty—where your article proposal is likely to be a one-time situation—I would quickly check the thesis sentence and lead in the features, write your query on that, and then go back to analyze it more thoroughly if you get a go-ahead for the article.

Can you sell reprints of a single article? Selling article reprints appears to be robust for some fields of writing and absolutely a dud for others. Because trade writing is so audience specific, it's very difficult to do a trade reprint per se. Consumer articles, on the whole, seem to do a brisker business in the reprint field, but again, not in every specialty. Like everything else, there are exceptions to this discouraging rule, even in trade magazines.

When we discuss trade periodical markets, we can't exclude association publications both national and regional. And related to these publications—often newsletters—are a variety of corporate publications designed to be read by either the corporation's employees or its clients or both.

While there is no hard and fast rule, two types of publications, association publications and corporate publications, are the most likely to use reprint material originally published in an independent trade magazine. Nowadays, these two types of publications often have on-line versions which increase your chances for reprint. But online publication also complicates the question of rights, which we will touch on a bit later. You *must* understand what rights you originally sold before you attempt any type of reprint sale.

Because trade magazine articles are so audience specific, you won't find as large a universe for reprints as you can with consumer articles. If you write a story about bed and breakfast establishments in the Seattle area, there truly is enough universal appeal in such a story to reprint to newspapers, customer and automotive magazines and newsletters, and even into the foreign markets, a subject covered by Michael Hedge in *The Writer's and Photographer's Guide to Global Markets.*

Three other variations are possible in trade article reprints. One writer I know has created his own form of self-syndication. His stories emphasize a wide array of personal skills that cut across industries: How to use the Internet. How to track business travel expenses. How to work a trade show effectively. How to deal with difficult co-workers. How to get the most out of your trade association. He writes an article a week or so and sends out a quarterly catalog to regional and local trade magazines and to associations. His prices are extremely reasonable for an editor who must work on little or no budget, and from what I understand, he earns a comfortable living working essentially two or three days a week.

But remember, it took more than ten years for him to build up to that level. Still, as a part-time endeavor, a self-syndication idea that can appeal across industry boundaries might be worth considering.

This variation, of course, begs the question: What's the dividing line between trade writing and general journalism that covers business. The dividing line, I would say, is a line that isn't necessary to have.

Many publications work at covering business in general—covering skills or techniques or events or issues that cut across industry boundaries. The distinction, if one is needed, is simple: You must have a grasp of general business principles to write for these publications. For specific trade magazines, you must have a grasp of general business principles plus a grasp of the specific issues and procedures affecting that particular industry. Since that understanding of general principles overlap, why would you exclude the general business press as potential markets?

And that's what the second variation is about. In the specific are the seeds of the general. I'll give you the start of your article's title: In the Details of a Specific Successful Project Can Be Found the Seeds of a New Way of Business. Taking the details of any specific project or process we cover should offer us fodder for metaphor and enlightenment about the larger business processes.

Take the jail again. The design firm on it, a well-known national firm, has learned not only how to spread the design out across the U.S. using Internet and intranet. Having also learned the Web knows no boundaries, it now has offices in other countries. When the jail was being designed, parts of the design were parceled out to offices spread out across the world. It was an interesting peak at a future which has become the present.

A final variation to garner extra money from your trade article research is to write a consumer version that can be sold across regional newspapers. If we take our earlier version of the jail's construction, for instance, we could put together a story on how communities can save money in jail construction. The piece might also focus on how the rising cost of such facilities is tying up tax money that could be used for safer schools and other necessary programs.

One jail I covered, for instance, will pay for its construction just through the savings in water use during the life of the facility. Using a unique vacuum flush system similar to those found on ships, the jail is saving more than 10,000 gallons per day in water. In thirty years, this daily savings amounts to the full cost of the project plus interest. As a taxpayer, I love it. As a writer, I have to share this information with as many places as possible. Don't be afraid to cross editorial borders if the topic has a universal potential. In this case, what saves water for one type of large institution housing many people may be of interest to other types of institutional housing managers such as managers of hospitals or college dormitories.

Sell it yourself or through a broker. The more you research a topic, the more you understand the needs of the audience that wants the information and the gaps in availability or presentation for the information.

One way to take additional advantage of the hard work you put in on the research is to publish a special report on a topics that either wasn't summarized conveniently for your target audience or was summarized so poorly as to render it virtually unreadable.

Another special report option: In the course of your research, you will come across experts who often have important knowledge to communicate but either don't have the time to write it down or don't have the skill to turn the information into an easily understood piece of writing. You can often work out an arrangement to collaborate with these individuals, and their knowledge of their industry will often be valuable in selecting ways and means to market a special report.

This collaboration can take different forms. In one case, you may become the "ghostwriter" of a special report the expert wants to market. In another case, you may become joint authors. Yet another method is to interview the expert and then publish the special report based on the interview.

Marketing special reports is a topic beyond the scope of this book. The special reports which seem to sell best are those which tell a reader how to do something, but reports that provide specific marketing information or deliver timely advice about capitalizing on the next trend in an industry can also be winners. Certainly how-to articles and books permeate our culture. As a trade writer, though, you will be developing very targeted how-to products. Using our jail story as an example, it would be possible to develop a report on how to design and build a jail that pays for itself. For another report, the manufacturers of the vacuum flush system could collaborate on a special report detailing how to design such a system and incorporate it into other types of buildings.

In this last instance, a more probably scenario would be to approach the manufacturer about preparing a case history or brochure which they can give to future customers. At this point, we have gone beyond writing for trade magazines and into the realm of corporate writing and public relations.

A quick aside. Straddling the line between freelance journalism and freelance public relations is tricky at best and at worst, working as a freelance public relations person can jeopardize your credibility with an editor. On the other hand, writing promotional copy often pays better than magazine writing.

The problem becomes one of perception. You may have high ethical standards, never mixing reportage with promotions, but once you begin writing promotional material, editors may look at you in a different light.

Another problem is more challenging and more personal: Will you lose your objectivity by crossing over into the world of promotional writing? Many editors believe it is impossible for a writer to do both types of writing, but my personal feeling is that it can be done. Not easily, however. It's one thing to intellectualize about remaining objective but quite another when you discover the developer who has been giving you lucrative promotional writing assignments is building his golf course over a tailings site.

The conflict of interest between objective reporting and promotional writing has more gray area than most people realize, and trade magazines, much more than consumer magazines, often blur the lines themselves. I don't find, however, that "straight" reporting is always as objective as advertised. We all have developed our biases. I don't believe Molly Ivins, whom I greatly admire, will bring the same point of view to a story about Sen. Orrin Hatch that William Buckley, Jr., whom I also admire, will bring. The biases creep in.

Is there a book?

Can you expand your special report into a book? Another very real possibility is that you wind up with enough research material for a full-length book. Your options are much the same as a special report: single authorship, collaboration, ghostwriting, and interview-based authorship.

Naturally you have several more options for getting a full-length book published. If you want to starve to death on the royalties, you can approach a mainline publisher. I don't mean to sound implacable, but the business of writing for a national book publishing company has deteriorated to a point where other options should be investigated first unless you have a clear "bestseller." It isn't worth your time to write for a publisher who is going to give you just 6% to 12% of the *net* on a book, which may be less than 55% of the cover, will do little to promote the book because it doesn't have a chance of being the next nonfiction million seller, and will expect you, in fact, to promote the book almost totally by yourself and at your own expense if it is to have any chance of selling.

Mid-size, independent publishers are a better option, I believe, because they have more soul invested in the books they publish than do the large houses. They also have considerably less budget for marketing, but the truth of the business is: If you are writing a book that caters to a specialized audience, the large and mid-sized publishing houses are not going to budget any more for promotion than a small independent would. Either way, you are going to spend quite a bit of your own time and money promoting your book if you want any sales, and much of your cost-effective marketing will be outside of the traditional bookstore. It's become a catchphrase among non-fiction writers that the way to make money with a book is to be a speaker, not an author.

This particular fact of life is one reason so many niche authors are now opting to self-publish and are finding that the barriers to doing so are becoming fewer and fewer. Since you end up spending your time and money to market if you want to have your book sell, why not spend a little more money so that you reap the entire profit? If this is an option you might consider, let me recommend you read Gordon Burgett's *Publishing to Niche Markets*. A niche publisher himself, Burgett offers sound advice about the key decisions a writer must make before self-publishing a nonfiction book to a narrow market segment. There is considerable literature developing on self-publishing, but for the trade writer, Burgett's book is the place to start.

Does your information have a global application?

Here's a secret. You *can* sell reprints to overseas magazines and periodicals. You can also sell reslanted articles if you are willing to invest the time and expense necessary to message back and forth across continents. Actually, e-mail and the World Wide Web have improved the cost-effectiveness of writing for markets overseas, but frankly the pay seldom justifies the effort.

Reprints, however, are different. To offer a reprint, you make several copies of the article at a copy shop. You then send these via snail mail to the various magazines you think would be candidates for such an article. Include a cover letter that states the availability of photos or transparencies and their format, the cost of the photos to the magazine, and a request to receive a tear sheet if the article is used.

Notice I didn't mention the fee you are charging for the reprint. You can specify a fee, of course, but most magazines have a set rate they will pay for reprints anyway, so if your fee is too high, your piece won't be used. If your fee is too low, you are cheating yourself.

Speaking of cheating, what's to keep the foreign publication from using your work without telling you? Absolutely nothing. Think about it though: If they wanted to pirate work, they can do so easily enough without you sending an article for consideration. You must trust the editor to be ethical until proven otherwise.

What about language differences? Simple enough to send a reprint written in American English to Australia, Britain, Ireland, and South Africa, but are you limited to the English-speaking countries solely unless you have the piece translated?

I'll pass along hearsay information at this point. I've never sold into a magazine that was printed in another language, but others tell me they have had little problem. English has become a lingua franca for the business and technical community around the world. As a result, most business magazines anywhere usually have at least one staff member who is fairly fluent in English, and most can have your article translated quickly.

This fact actually opens up additional avenues. Because you want to avoid overlapping jurisdictions when you are selling reprint rights, you must take precautions not to allow competitive markets to print your article at the same time. Not only is this fair copyright practice, it is also a terrible mistake in terms of getting future articles considered.

But, just because two magazines operate within the same geographical area doesn't necessarily mean they compete with each other. One difference can be language. You can offer one, say, the right to publish your article in English to one while you offer another the right to publish the article in Spanish. Does this situation come up? Apparently so, although I have no direct experience with it. Asia and Europe appear to be the areas where this kind of situation opens up opportunity. You could, for instance, be doing an article on oil exploration in the North Sea where a reprint would make sense for both a British trade magazine that is read throughout Europe and a Norwegian magazine that is read primarily in Scandinavian countries.

On the other hand, common sense says to be wary. If the trade magazine in English is widely read in the Scandinavian countries, you may want to offer a reslanted version to the Norwegian magazine to make both happier.

The second piece of hearsay. European countries, with the exception of France, and Asian countries with the exception of mainland China except for high-tech pieces, are the most amenable to reprinting articles from the U.S. If the topic is Canadian, or at least perceived to be generated from there, the reception in France and in Latin American countries improves considerably.

Now the basic practice in the U.S. and Canada is to sell "First North American serial rights" to a periodical publica-

198

tion. To be honest, there is absolutely no legal reason to wait until your article is published in the U.S. before you try selling overseas if you have sold the article in the U.S. under these rights.

As a practical matter, I believe your chance of selling the article is actually better as a reprint than it is as a first piece. If you can mention the article was published or is being published in a prestigious American trade magazine, it gets more consideration than a virginal unsolicited manuscript.

Whatever other faults, the U.S. and Canada are among the world's leaders in the development and refinement of technology and business techniques. Because of that situation, an article generated for and coming from those climes has just a bit more provenance than the average article in a wide variety of topics.

Another consideration, however, is that many U.S. megapublishers print and publish foreign editions. It's more and more possible to sell an article to a U.S. trade publication and then sell a reprint to a foreign trade magazine that competes with the U.S. publication's sister. With so much more potential to appear in international and even transnational markets, thanks to the World Wide Web, it is also imperative that both you and the publisher are agreed on what rights are being sold.

Embarrassing situations are beginning to proliferate, such as selling a reprint to a foreign publication and then finding it published the same month in an international edition of a domestic publication. When that happens, you had better know what rights you sold. Almost more important, however, is whether you will be able to smooth the situation over with the two competing editors.

How much can you expect to make from foreign reprint sales? The results I have heard about vary significantly. Based on a very unofficial and unprofessional straw pole, computer and medical writers do the best with the overseas markets and have made up $2000 extra through overseas reprints. At the other end of the spectrum, some writers have poured dollar after dollar into international stamps with no results whatsoever.

Michael H. Sedge's book, mentioned earlier, offers information and practical advice on the mechanics of working the foreign markets although his focus is primarily on consumer, not trade, markets. But the information on the sales process and the physical process of transmitting articles and photos is applicable to both.

As this book is being written, the way articles are marketed and transmitted is changing rapidly for both the domestic and foreign markets. Email, particularly, is becoming more and more acceptable for queries, article transmission, and even for transmitting photography and illustrations.

With the advent of the Internet, however, copyright considerations that were of little concern before are pushing to the forefront for writers.

How do copyright laws affect you in a rapidly changing industry?

We've mentioned how the Internet situation is increasing the potential for an article, but also the potential to be exploited or embarassed. Perhaps the single biggest difficulty in copyright law for articles now revolves around the interpretation of what "first rights" adds up to. Twenty years ago, when you sent an article to a magazine and had it accepted as first rights, the magazine would publish it once and then you were free to do what you wanted with it unless you had also granted some future rights such as the right to include the piece in an anthology.

With few exceptions, rights in the U.S. and Canada were essentially "First North American rights in English." In other words, the publisher had the right to publish the material in English once in North America. All other rights you retained.

As the catch phrase from *Monty Python's Flying Circus* succinctly puts it: "And now, for something completely different." The World Wide Web.

Trade magazine publishers increasingly are putting their

issues on-line. Unfortunately, some of them do so without securing the rights from the author. On-line, of course, also means that the article is available beyond the boundaries of North America, so they are paying for North American rights, but using the material on a worldwide basis without giving the author additional compensation.

Or are they? One argument floating around goes like this: When the server for these on-line editions is based in North America, then it is a North American edition. If someone from France happens by to read it on-line, it is no different than if a copy migrated to France in the suitcase of a vendor.

What's more to the point, though, is that the publisher is using the article in two different venues while compensating the writer for only one. In the wake of a backlash from writers, some publishers now insist on all rights while still paying a pittance for the article. This puts the writer in a difficult situation, especially as you gain experience in reselling your work.

What should you do in this situation? No hard and fast rule applies. If you think your article has terrific resale potential, then perhaps your best course is to withdraw the article or toughen negotiations until you get the dough you think it could earn. If a reslant and rewrite would have the same potential, then perhaps you should go ahead and agree.

Because the legal situation for intellectual property is so gray nowadays, one of the best investments a writer can make is membership in the National Writers Union which actively pursues the interests of writers through both legislation and litigation.

Now, another situation that is developing is the increase in "e-zines" that deal with business and trade subjects. An interesting observation: The generation gap between old and young is now most notable by the way they read. As we get ready for the year 2000, studies are showing that the under-30 crowd is at ease with reading their information solely from a computer screen while the over 30 age group almost always wants a printed copy. Here is the implication.

Although trade magazines are available on-line, most do

not yet publish the full content that normally goes into print versions. As the population ages, however, and the under-30 moves into their 40's and 50's when they begin to take the reins of business and industry, I fully expect to see this trend reverse. As the trend shifts, so will the publishers' insistence on "all rights" or a minimum of "all electronic rights and first North American serial print rights." Why "all electronic"? While I don't believe we will ever become a paperless society, I can see a future where trade magazines come on something like a CD-ROM to be plugged into a universal reader.

I believe the paperless trend in magazine production will come as quickly as large publishers determine what is acceptable as a standard reader. Let's be honest, publishing is driven by revenues and expenses just like any other business. CD-ROM production has become so much less expensive than print production—and the attendant storage and mailing costs are much less as well—that I'm a bit surprised magazine publishers have waited this long—but that's another book.

Ah, but what if you can print from the CD-ROM? Well, of course you can. Doesn't that open up another right to be protected as well? You bet it does. What if you can print a copy of the article from the web site? Of course you can, and I think that's a right protection that has been given short shrift as well.

All of which is turning writers into amateur lawyers. I wish I had answers, but I don't. My best advice in this realm: Learn the basics from a good book (see appendix). Join the National Writers Union. Look for an on-line discussion of copyright laws. Read every contract you are offered all the way through. Find a good copyright lawyer who can advise you on difficult situations. If the train is about to run over you, you at least have a chance to step out of the way if you see it coming, but almost no chance if you simply close your eyes.

Start building your career

Well, there you have all the advice I have to give for now. All I can add is that trade journalism has been an unexpected joy which has opened opportunities to meet people and to learn about interesting ideas and techniques not only for a single industry, but also for life in general.

The only other suggestion I can offer is to plunge into the field with care. This is an area of the writing business where it is perfectly possible, even preferable, to stick your toe into the water before diving in. Building contacts, both at magazines and within the industry you cover, is paramount to your success. This network won't happen overnight. Even if you are a retired industry professional who already has a wide range of industry contacts, the relationships you need to build with magazine editors will take time and not a little patience.

But if you have that patience, I can guarantee that this field offers a tremendous opportunity to add to your full-time or retirement income as well as an opportunity to have more fun in the writing than you expect.

Bibliography

Clinton, Patrick. *Guide to Writing for the Business Press.* NTC Publishing Group: 1997. A very thorough discussion of both writing and editorial strategies and tactics for trade magazines. Highly recommended if you are serious about a long-term career in business journalism.

Canton, Al. *The Silver Pen: Starting a Profitable Writing Business from a Lifetime of Experience: A Guide for Older People.* Adams Blake Publishing Co.: 1996.
Don't let the title fool you, there is a wealth of information on a business-like approach to the writing profession in this book for young people as well. Canton's approach, although not targeted just to trade magazine journalism, offers good advice for those who have thought about trying to write but were too busy developing skills in other areas during their main working life.

Brande, Dorothea and John Gardner. *Becoming a Writer.* J.P. Tarcher: 1981.
Why recommend a book geared toward fiction? Because Dorothea Brande 1930's classic doesn't talk about technique but about how to get on with the most difficult problem in writing: motivating yourself day after day to not only write, but write well.

Kent, Peter. *Making Money in Technical Writing.* Arco: 1997.
Although Peter Kent's book is about the unique field of technical writing, his concise but detailed advice on how to manage the administrative and marketing aspects of a writing business is some of the useful advice I've ever seen. Highly recommended, not just for the advice but also because it's a good example of how a potentially dry subject becomes vivid and lively in the hands of a skilled writer.

Sedge, Michael H. *The Writer's and Photographer's Guide to Global Markets.* 1998.

Although geared to consumer journalism, Sedge's book will help you understand how to approach marketing to magazines outside the U.S. The world of trade magazines is driven by business, and business is definitely global, so the opportunities available to trade journalists aren't bound by the borders of North America.

SIDE TRIPS

Inevitably, as you progress in the trade journalism arena, you will be approached to work on business projects outside the strict arena of trade journalism. These books will help you decide if you want to do such publications and if you do, how to make the transition successfully.

Fisher, Lionel L. *The Craft of Corporate Journalism: Writing and Editing Creative Organizational Publications.* 1992.

Sorenson, George. *Writing for the Corporate Market: How to Make Big Money Freelancing for Business.* 1990.

With continued acquisitions and mergers, and the consequent downsizing and restructuring of corporate communications departments, Sorenson's advice on how to become the outsourced resource for public relations and other kinds of corporate writing is even more pertinent today.

INDEX

209

FIND A MAGAZINE TO WRITE FOR AT THE TRADE WRITER'S RESOURCE CENTER

Kendall Hanson has set up a web site to make it easier for freelancers to get information they need about the trade magazine industry.

The Trade Writer's Resource Center, a free service located at **http://tradewriter.freeservers.com**, has links to individual online trade magazines, categorized by industry, to make it easier for writers to find new markets and to keep track of editorial staff changes.

The site also has links to the major trade magazine publishing houses, links to the main writing and professional associations for trade journalists, links to job sites for freelance writers and journalists, links to freelance writing resource sites such as About.com and Suite 101, and links to news about the magazine industry so writers can stay abreast of the acquisitions, reorganizations, and rapid changes that affect this exciting industry.

At the site writers can also subscribe to Kendall Hanson's monthly online newsletter, *Serious Business*, which focuses the magazines produced by one major trade publishing house each month, has articles on improving writing and marketing skills, news of happenings in the trade magazine industry, and news and information for writers and editors seeking jobs in the industry.

"I urge writers who are serious about producing articles for the trade magazine industry to start their search for markets at my site. I began the work originally because I was making so many 'bookmarks' on my own browser that I was overloading my computer. Trade journalism has been good to me, so it seemed only natural to want to share the information I've gained."

FIND WHAT YOU NEED AT
http://tradewriter.freeservers.com

LOOK FOR THESE UPCOMING BOOKS FROM DIXON-PRICE PUBLISHING!

A THOUSAND MILES IN THE ROB ROY CANOE

"The sound of a railway train beside the river reminds you that this is not quite a strange, wild, unseen country. Reminds you, I say, because really when you are in the river bed you easily forget all that is beyond each side. Let a landscape be ever so well known from the road, it becomes new again when you view it from the level of the water."

Written by the adventurous John MacGregor, this book launched the modern recreational sports of canoe camping and sea kayaking. Follow MacGregor through mid-19th Century Europe as he paddles and sails the plucky Rob Roy decked canoe down the Thames into the English Channel and then on to the famous rivers of the Continent.

       Paperback   ISBN: 1-929516-06-1
       Electronic   ISBN: 1-929516-01-0

A BEACHCOMBER IN THE ORIENT

"Where do we go?" demanded the poet.

"Wherever they take us."

We climbed into two of the carriages and away we went . . . Wherever they were going, it became evident that they were not going into town; the road became a path and finally a mere trail, the trees became a tangle of palms and banana trees. The golden moon, seeping though the jungle growth, shed an eerie light in mysterious patches upon the glistening bodies of the Annamites, and still they trotted, untiring, turning corners until we had lost all sense of direction, to pause finally before an atap-shack half-hidden among the profuse vines, where they indicated by gesture that we were to dismount.

"*Bien*," said the poet, a trifle doubtfully. "We see what is this place."

Before there was Hunter S. Thompson, there was Harry L. Foster, a "gonzo" journalist who roamed the world seeking, and finding, adventure. Often penniless, Foster worked odd jobs and the occasional scam as he made his way in and out of comic and sometimes tragic situations, but always observing his fellow man and himself with humor and insight.

       Paperback   ISBN: 1-929516-09-6
       Electronic   ISBN: 1-929516-04-5

Find them at www.dixonprice.com